Beginning Ionic Mobile Development

Greg Lim

COPYRIGHT © 2017 BY GREG LIM

FIRST EDITION: JULY 2017

CONTENTS

Preface

About this book

Ionic is one of the leading frameworks to develop mobile apps and Progressive Web Apps in HTML5. Ionic is especially useful if you are familiar with web development HTML, CSS, JavaScript and would like to build mobile apps, but don't fancy having to learn Objective C and/or Swift for iOS, Java for Android, etc.

In this book, we take you on a fun, hands-on and pragmatic journey to master Ionic. You'll start building Ionic apps within minutes. Every section is written in a bite-sized manner and straight to the point as I don't want to waste your time (and most certainly mine) on the content you don't need. In the end, you will have what it takes to develop a real-life mobile app using Ionic.

Requirements

Basic familiarity with HTML, CSS, Javascript and Angular.

Contact and Code Examples

Please address comments and questions concerning this book to support@i-ducate.com.

Code examples can be obtained by going to my GitHub repository at https://github.com/greglim81/ so if you don't want to type in the code examples from this book, do visit the repository and get the code there.

Chapter 1: Introduction to Ionic

In this book, we will learn how to create mobile apps with the Ionic framework (or simply known as Ionic). With Ionic, you can create high quality mobile apps using familiar web technologies like HTML, CSS and JavaScript. You can publish a mobile app on different mobile platforms (web, Android, iOS) with a **single code base** and do not have to painstakingly use the native tools for each platform e.g.:

- creating Android apps in Java using Android Studio
- creating iOS apps with Objective C or Swift using Xcode
- creating mobile websites with html, css and JavaScript

With a single code HTML, CSS, Javascript base, you can publish Android, iOS and web mobile apps (or progressive web apps) simultaneously.

In addition, Ionic makes it easy for you to design your interface. It provides user interface components like the tab bar, side menu, etc which do not exist as native HTML elements. Ionic extends the HTML library to create these and they look behave like the native controls to provide native-like experience.

Built on Top of Angular

Ionic is built on top of other technologies and this course assumes basic knowledge of HTML, CSS and JavaScript. Angular is the underlying framework that powers Ionic. Because Angular is quite a big topic by itself, I have written a separate book on it. I strongly recommend learning Angular before starting this course. But as a quick summary, Angular is a framework to build complex single page applications and Ionic leverages the power this framework offers. For example, Ionic's components are simply Angular components.

Ionic apps uses TypeScript for its code. If you are unfamiliar with Typescript, don't worry. I assure you that it is easy to pick up. It is essentially a typed superset of Javascript that compiles to plain Javascript, so its not a completely new language.

You can develop Ionic apps on MacOS, Windows or Linux. Just be aware that to compile iOS apps, you need to work on MacOS.

Going Through This Book

We will guide you through the process of writing an application from start, how to use Ionic visual components, styles, add pages, navigate between those pages, and more. We will then learn how to build and run our apps on Android, iOS and deploy them onto the different App stores.

We will see how to store data persistently in the device using the Ionic *Storage* library. We will also see how to manage data remotely and implement login authentication/authorization using Firebase.

Finally, we will see how to use native mobile APIs to add native functionality features not normally available to web applications (e.g. Camera, GPS, Maps) but which we can access in our Android and iOS apps.

Required Tools

Before you can start developing with Ionic, you will need the following tools.

- A computer running Windows, MacOS, or Linux.

- The Chrome Web Browser. You can use another browser if you prefer, but we will use the Chrome Developer Tools a lot, so it's easier if you use Chrome.

- A text editor or IDE, preferably with TypeScript support. In this book, we use Visual Studio Code. It's cross-platform, free and open source. But you can use whichever IDE you prefer. Other popular choices include Atom, Sublime Text and Visual Studio IDE.

- Node.js, because it includes *npm*, a tool used to install JavaScript packages. Go to the Node website at nodejs.org and download the installer for your development platform.

- It will be good to also have access to both an Android and iOS mobile device to install and test your application on. While the iOS and Android provide emulators, they are no substitute for testing on a real device.

Installing Ionic CLI and Cordova

Ionic apps are created and developed primarily through the Ionic Command Line (CLI for short) and uses Cordova to build and deploy as a native app. Cordova provides the interface between the WebView and the device's native layer, to bridge the gap between the two (hence the original name of PhoneGap).

You will need to install the latest version of Ionic CLI and Cordova. Before you can do that, you will need a recent version of Node.js (as of time of writing, install Node.js 6 or greater). Once Node.js has been installed, run the following command in the Terminal to install the latest version of the Ionic CLI:

```
npm install -g ionic
```

For Mac users, you may encounter issues with permissions during the installation. If that happens, rerun the command with *sudo* as preface as shown below.

```
sudo npm install -g ionic
```

This allows the command to run as the root user. Note that *npm* stands for Node Package Manager. *npm* is used to perform the installation of the Ionic CLI. The installation should take some time to complete. Once the Ionic CLI installation is complete, check it by issuing the *ionic –v* command in the Terminal to list the version of Ionic you have just installed.

Next, we will next install Cordova also via *npm*. To install Cordova, run

```
npm install -g ionic cordova
```

*again you may need *sudo* if permission is denied to access certain folders during installation

To check the installation, enter *cordova –v* to list the version you have just installed.

Summary

In this chapter, we learned that Ionic, built on top of Angular, allows us to develop mobile applications for different platforms all with a single code base. We covered the required tools to use Ionic, and the steps to install Ionic CLI and Cordova. Now, proceed on to the next chapter to start creating your first Ionic app!

CHAPTER 2: SETTING UP OUR DEVELOPMENT ENVIRONMENT

Introduction

In this chapter, we will create our first Ionic app. We will learn how to create a project and how to use add Ionic components to it. We will create a Note taking app called *NotableNotes* that allows user to list, add, delete and edit notes to illustrate the standard C.R.U.D. (Create, Read, Update, Delete) operations.

Starting a New Ionic App

The first step is to create a new project. We can create a new project by running the below command in the Ionic CLI in Terminal, but first make sure that you are in the folder where you want to keep your Ionic projects.

```
ionic start <project folder name>
```

We can also pass in a *template* option to create a project with a template. i.e.

```
ionic start <project folder name> <template name>
```

Ionic has a few templates available:
- *tabs*
- *sidemenu*
- *blank*

If you don't specify a template, by default the *tabs* template will be used.

For most of our examples, we will use the blank template which is a basic Ionic app with a single page.

In our case type:

```
ionic start NotableNotes blank
```

The CLI will download the template and configure various components. It may ask you if you wish to create an Ionic.io account, but we can ignore that for now. Once done, Ionic CLI will have created a new folder called *NotableNotes*. Along with creating our project, *ionic start* also installs *npm* modules for the application and sets up Cordova for our project.

Viewing the App in a Browser

In the Terminal, *cd* into the folder that was created. To get a quick preview of our app in the browser, run

```
ionic serve
```

This will open a new browser showing the welcome message as seen below (fig. 2.1).

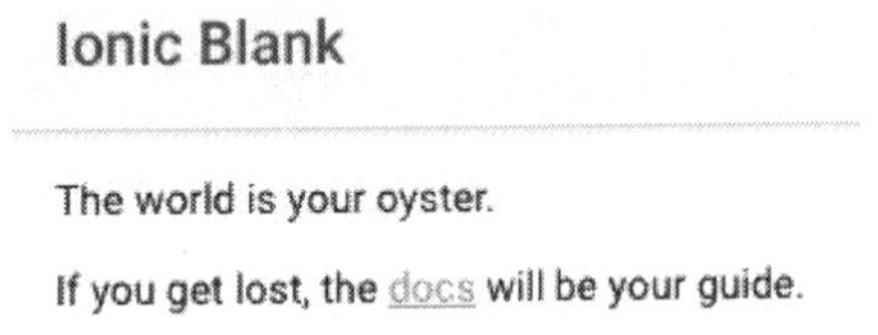

Ionic Blank

The world is your oyster.

If you get lost, the docs will be your guide.

figure 2.1

The *ionic serve* command runs the application locally in a browser. It starts a simple web server, opens our browser and loads the application for us. It also listens to file changes and auto-refresh the browser whenever a file is saved.

Being able to run our application on a browser is a huge advantage as development and testing done in the browser is much faster and productive especially when making code changes. Developing a traditional native application would require that we compile our application and then run it in an emulator or deploy it on an actual device every time we make a code change.

Project Structure

Now, let's go over the project structure created by the *ionic start* command. We won't explain what each single folder and file is for (that will be quite boring). We will learn more about each file and folder gradually through the course. For now, we will focus on the `src` folder. This is where we spend most of our time changing and adding application code.

Our code files consists of raw and uncompiled TypeScript code. When we run *ionic serve*, these code gets transpiled into the correct Javascript version that the browser understands.

In *src*, we have the *pages* folder that contains a *home* folder which has three files in it (home.html, home.scss, home.ts – stands for typescript). home.html contains what we see in the browser as shown below:

```
<ion-header>
  <ion-navbar>
    <ion-title>
       Ionic Blank
    </ion-title>
  </ion-navbar>
</ion-header>

<ion-content padding>
  The world is your oyster.
  <p>
    If you get lost, the <a href="http://ionicframework.com/docs/v2">docs</a>
will be your guide.
  </p>
</ion-content>
```

home.html contains Ionic specific tags like *ion-header, ion-navbar* and so on. All these tags are simply Angular components provided by Ionic. They start with the `ion` prefix so its easy to distinguish them from our own components. We will look at Ionic components in detail over time. For now, try changing the title in *home.html* to 'Notable Notes' as shown:

```
<ion-header>
  <ion-navbar>
    <ion-title>
      Notable Notes
    </ion-title>
  </ion-navbar>
</ion-header>
```

When you save this file, the app reloads automatically and you see the new title displayed in the header. This automatic refresh is taken care of by the *ionic serve* command we have running in the Terminal. *home.html* as introduced earlier is the template of the home component defined in *home.ts* as shown below:

```
import { Component } from '@angular/core';
import { NavController } from 'ionic-angular';

@Component({
  selector: 'page-home',
  templateUrl: 'home.html'
})
export class HomePage {

  constructor(public navCtrl: NavController) {

  }

}
```

Notice that it has a *@Component* just like any Angular component. The class name is HomePage and it uses home.html as its template. An Ionic page is basically an Angular component. It represents a screen in our application. In Ionic, they are called *pages* by convention. In the constructor, we have the Ionic navigation controller *NavController* which we use to navigate between pages. We will cover navigation later.

app

In *app* folder, you see *app.component.ts*. This is the root component of our application.

```
import { Component } from '@angular/core';
import { Platform } from 'ionic-angular';
import { StatusBar } from '@ionic-native/status-bar';
import { SplashScreen } from '@ionic-native/splash-screen';

import { HomePage } from '../pages/home/home';
@Component({
```

```
  templateUrl: 'app.html'
})
export class MyApp {
  rootPage:any = HomePage;

  constructor(platform: Platform, statusBar: StatusBar, splashScreen:
SplashScreen) {
    platform.ready().then(() => {
      // Okay, so the platform is ready and our plugins are available.
      // Here you can do any higher level native things you might need.
      statusBar.styleDefault();
      splashScreen.hide();
    });
  }
}
```

It is an app component called *MyApp*. Its template is stored in *app.html* as shown below. All these are simply Angular concepts.

```
<ion-nav [root]="rootPage"></ion-nav>
```

Now note that *app.html* uses the *ion-nav* component. The *root* property is binded to *rootPage* that is set to *HomePage* back in *app.component.ts*. This sets the root page to *HomePage*. If you are familiar with Angular router, you can think of *ion-nav* as *router-outlet*. In an Ionic app, we don't use the Angular router because Ionic provides its own navigation mechanism designed specifically for mobile applications.

App Module

We also have App Module in *src/app/app.module.ts* like any Angular application.

```
import { BrowserModule } from '@angular/platform-browser';
import { ErrorHandler, NgModule } from '@angular/core';
import { IonicApp, IonicErrorHandler, IonicModule } from 'ionic-angular';
import { SplashScreen } from '@ionic-native/splash-screen';
import { StatusBar } from '@ionic-native/status-bar';

import { MyApp } from './app.component';
import { HomePage } from '../pages/home/home';

@NgModule({
  declarations: [
    MyApp,
    HomePage
```

```
  ],
  imports: [
    BrowserModule,
    IonicModule.forRoot(MyApp)
  ],
  bootstrap: [IonicApp],
  entryComponents: [
    MyApp,
    HomePage
  ],
  providers: [
    StatusBar,
    SplashScreen,
    {provide: ErrorHandler, useClass: IonicErrorHandler}
  ]
})
export class AppModule {}
```

App Module is our root module that controls the rest of the application.

Like a typical Angular app, we have the *NgModule* decorator. For Ionic however, in *imports*, we use the IonicModule instead of BrowserModule and we pass MyApp (our root component) into *forRoot* method of IonicModule. IonicModule is imported from *ionic-angular*, the package that contains all the Ionic functionality.

Also, we bootstrap IonicApp Component imported from *ionic-angular* module. We don't need to worry too much about the details, because the Ionic CLI generates all these boiler plate for us. What we need to understand here is that an Ionic app is basically an Angular application with a few differences like added custom Ionic Modules and Components.

In fact, if we look at the *main.ts* file, its uses *platformBrowserDynamic* to bootstrap our AppModule exactly like an Angular web application.

```
import { platformBrowserDynamic } from '@angular/platform-browser-dynamic';

import { AppModule } from './app.module';

platformBrowserDynamic().bootstrapModule(AppModule);
```

index.html

src/index.html is the main entry point of our app which main purpose is to setup *script*, CSS, *bootstrap* and start running our app. Ionic looks for the *<ion-app>* tag shown in **bold** below to render our application:

```html
<!DOCTYPE html>
<html lang="en" dir="ltr">
<head>
  <meta charset="UTF-8">
  <title>Ionic App</title>
  <meta name="viewport" content="width=device-width, initial-scale=1.0, minimum-scale=1.0, maximum-scale=1.0, user-scalable=no">
  <meta name="format-detection" content="telephone=no">
  <meta name="msapplication-tap-highlight" content="no">

  <link rel="icon" type="image/x-icon" href="assets/icon/favicon.ico">
  <link rel="manifest" href="manifest.json">
  <meta name="theme-color" content="#4e8ef7">

  <!-- cordova.js required for cordova apps -->
  <script src="cordova.js"></script>

  <!-- un-comment this code to enable service worker -->
  <script>
    if ('serviceWorker' in navigator) {
      navigator.serviceWorker.register('service-worker.js')
        .then(() => console.log('service worker installed'))
        .catch(err => console.log('Error', err));
    }
  </script>-->

  <link href="build/main.css" rel="stylesheet">

</head>
<body>

  <!-- Ionic's root component and where the app will load -->
  <ion-app></ion-app>

  <!-- The polyfills js is generated during the build process -->
  <script src="build/polyfills.js"></script>

  <!-- The bundle js is generated during the build process -->
  <script src="build/main.js"></script>

</body>
</html>
```

We don't have to worry about how exactly *index.html* works because its taken care by the Ionic scripts. The important thing to note is that we have the *ion-app* tag. *ion-app* is the selector that matches the ionic app component which we bootstrap in our app module. So an Ionic app always has *ion-app* in its *index.html* where the application will be rendered.

Summary

In this chapter, we built a first Ionic test app and previewed it locally in our browser. We have a basic walkthrough of the project structure of an Ionic app, how to use Ionic components and have a better understanding of the key elements that make up a single Ionic screen. At this point, we will know enough about our project to add our own functionality which we will do in the next chapter.

CHAPTER 3: BUILDING OUR NOTABLE NOTES APP

In this chapter, we will begin building our NotableNotes app. We will implement the fetching of notes, using Ionic components to list them and creating of a note detail page to show the note.

To begin, first locate and open the NotableNotes folder in VScode (or your favorite IDE).

3.1 Listing Notes

In our home page, we want to display a list of notes. We begin by defining some dummy note objects in an array *notes* in *home.ts*. Add the lines in **bold**.

```
import { Component } from '@angular/core';
import { NavController } from 'ionic-angular';

@Component({
  selector: 'page-home',
  templateUrl: 'home.html'
})
export class HomePage {

  constructor(public navCtrl: NavController) {
  }

  notes = [
    {
      id: '1',
      date: '2016-01-01', //yyyy-mm-dd
      title: 'Ionic 2',
      content: 'Learn the basics of Ionic 2.'
    },
    {
      id: '2',
      date: '2016-02-01',
      title: 'Firebase',
      content: 'A great backend for Ionic applications'
    },
    {
      id: '3',
      date: '2016-03-01',
      title: 'Angular',
```

```
        content: 'A good grasp of it is crucial to developing great Ionic 2
apps.'
      }
  ];

}
```

We declared a *notes* array that contains three *note* objects. Each *note* object has properties *id*, *date*, *title* and *content*.

Next, we define the template of HomePage in home.html as shown below.

home.html

```
<ion-header>
  <ion-navbar>
    <ion-title>
      Notable Notes
    </ion-title>
  </ion-navbar>
</ion-header>

<ion-content padding>
  <ion-card *ngFor="let note of notes">
    <ion-card-header>
      {{ note.date }}
    </ion-card-header>
    <ion-card-content>
      <ion-card-title>
        {{ note.title }}
      </ion-card-title>
      <p>
        {{ note.content }}
      </p>
    </ion-card-content>
  </ion-card>
</ion-content>
```

Code Explanation

In home.html, we make use of the *ion-card* Ionic component. As defined in the Ionic docs, "Cards are a great way to display important pieces of content, and are quickly emerging as a core design pattern for apps…".

The Ionic docs illustrate how to use the Card component (fig. 3.1.1), and even provides an image of a mobile device on the right side to show how it will look on a mobile device.

Basic Usage   Demo Source

Cards are primarily a CSS component. To use a basic card, follow this structure:

```
<ion-card>

  <ion-card-header>
    Card Header
  </ion-card-header>

  <ion-card-content>
    <!-- Add card content here! -->
  </ion-card-content>

</ion-card>
```

figure 3.1.1

The Ionic docs provide a valuable resource on how to use Ionic components and it will benefit you if you refer to it frequently. For example, we can read more about the *cards* component at https://ionicframework.com/docs/components/#cards.

Using *ngFor*, we render an ion-card element for each *note* in *notes* with `*ngFor="let note of notes"`.

Next, using interpolation, we render *date* in *ion-card-header* with `{{ note.date }}`. We similarly render *title* in *ion-card-title* and *content* in *ion-card-content*.

Running your Application

When you run your application, you should get something like in figure 3.1.2:

21

Notable Notes

2016-01-01

Ionic 2

Learn the basics of Ionic 2.

2016-02-01

Firebase

A great backend for Ionic applications

2016-03-01

Angular

A good grasp of it is crucial to developing great Ionic 2 apps.

figure 3.1.2

As mentioned in the Ionic docs, "cards are a great way to display important pieces of content, and are quickly emerging as a core design pattern for apps…Cards have fast become the design pattern of choice for many companies, including the likes of Google, Twitter, and Spotify."

Notice how easy it is to use the visually appealing and recognizable UI elements provided by Ionic!

The Importance of Using Ionic Components

Ionic automatically apply different styles depending on each platform our app is running on. This feature plays a big part in making sure that our app looks like a native mobile app. This also shows us how it is important to use Ionic components whenever possible, e.g. *ion-header*, *ion-content* rather than standard html elements because Ionic automatically adapts to the platform we are running on.

3.2 Applying Pipes

Pipes are useful in formatting values, like converting a number into a currency representation or dates into a human-readable format. Pipes are not something new in Ionic, rather they are part of Angular which comes with a set of commonly used pipes like DatePipe, UpperCasePipe, LowerCasePipe and CurrencyPipe.

In our application, our date is currently shown as 2016-01-01. But if we were to apply the date pipe as shown below:

```
<ion-card-header>
  {{ note.date | date }}
</ion-card-header>
```

our date would be formatted as Jan 1, 2016.

Jan 1, 2016

Ionic 2

Learn the basics of Ionic 2.

If we had a currency property, we can use the use Angular currency pipe. You can read more about the currency pipe documentation at
https://angular.io/docs/ts/latest/api/common/index/CurrencyPipe-pipe.html

3.3 Clickable Items

Next, we will implement clicking on an item and opening another page where we display details for that note and edit it. Add the *click* event handler as shown below in **bold**.

```
<ion-card *ngFor="let note of notes" (click)="onItemClick(note)">
```

Events in Angular use the parentheses notation. i.e. *(click)*. This will trigger the *onItemClick()* method in the home.ts component. We thus have to implement *onItemClick()* in home.ts as shown below:

```
...
export class HomePage {,
```

23

```
...
onItemClick(note){
    console.log("item-click",note);
}
}
```

When we run the app now and click on a note, you can see the *note* object being printed to the console (figure 3.3.1). To view the console, in Chrome, go to *View*, *Developer*, *Developer Tools*, and go to the *console* tab.

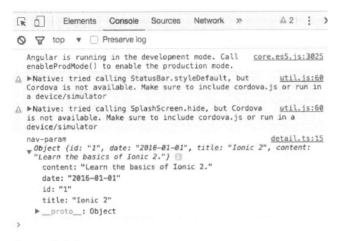

figure 3.3.1

Note: In the developer console, you will see a warning saying, "…Cordova is not available". This is expected because we are running our app with *ionic serve* on a browser whereas cordova is only available when we run our app on iOS or Android as a proper mobile app. We will cover more about cordova later in the course.

3.4 Adding a New Page

We will now see how to create a new page and how to navigate to that page when we click on an item in the list.

To add a page, navigate to your app project folder and type the command:

```
ionic g page <name of page>
```

In our case we will name our new page *detail* since it contains the details of our note. So the command should be:

```
ionic g page detail
```

The command creates a new *detail* folder in the *src/app/pages* folder with four new files, detail.html, detail.module.ts, detail.scss and detail.ts. Let's go through the page structure.

Page Structure

detail.module.ts

In Ionic 3, each new page is by default setup as a separate module in order to implement lazy loading of pages. Lazy loading in essence is taking one segment of code, a chunk, and loading it on demand as the app requests it so that the application loads much faster. As apps start to grow, lazy loading pages becomes much more important. If your app has 50 over different pages and many more UI components, loading these all up front is very resource expensive. Instead, if you can only load 2-4 different components up front and lazy load the rest, users will have a much better experience.

In our app, the new page will be declared in detail.module.ts as shown below.

```
import { NgModule } from '@angular/core';
import { IonicPageModule } from 'ionic-angular';
import { Detail } from './detail';

@NgModule({
  declarations: [
    Detail,
  ],
  imports: [
    IonicPageModule.forChild(Detail),
  ],
  exports: [
    Detail
  ]
})
export class DetailModule {}
```

detail.ts

In our component detail.ts, the *@IonicPage()* decorator will have been added above the component decorator.

```
import { Component } from '@angular/core';
import { IonicPage, NavController, NavParams } from 'ionic-angular';

@IonicPage()
@Component({
  selector: 'page-detail',
  templateUrl: 'detail.html',
})
export class Detail {
  ...
}
```

Pushing our Page

With this way of adding in Ionic 3, you no longer have to add imports to *detail* outside of the *detail* module. You also don't have to declare *detail* in app.module.ts.

To navigate from home.ts to detail.ts, we need to use the NavController class that we import in home.ts. Its a service provided by Ionic which is injected into the constructor as shown below.

```
export class HomePage {

  constructor(public navCtrl: NavController) {
  }
  ...
}
```

We call the *push* method of navCtrl and give it the string 'Detail' (the name used in *declarations* array of detail.module.ts).

```
onItemClick(note){
  this.navCtrl.push('Detail');
}
```

*Unlike in Ionic 2, in Ionic 3 we no longer give the imported class when pushing the page in NavController.

NavController is similar to Angular router but a lot simpler. To go to another page, we call *navCtrl push* and we pass the destination page string. Why is the method called *push*? The NavController keeps a navigation stack that has multiple pages stacked upon one another. When our app starts, we display our home page. So initially, the navigation stack contains a single page which is home. When we navigate to *detail* page, we push *detail* onto the stack.

So detail page is displayed because it's on the top of the stack. But the home page is still there underneath. And when we go back from detail page (by clicking on the back button), we pop the detail page from the stack which reveals the home page again. We currently have two pages at the moment but a real world application would have several more pages pushed on the stack, and then navigate back and forth between them.

Running our App

If you run your app now, click on any note and the detail page appears. Note that the detail page provides a back button provided by Ionic automatically. When we click on it, it pops the detail off the navigation stack making the home page visible.

Note that there is also a transition effect when we navigate from one page to another. Ionic provides this so that our app looks like a native app. The animation style differs depending on the platform.

3.5 Navigation Parameters

Now, we will make our detail page display information from a specific note. The NavController push method accepts an additional second argument called *params*. We can use this argument to pass in any data we need from the current page to the page we are navigating to. In our case, we pass in a *note* object by adding the codes in bold below.

home.ts

```
onItemClick(note){
  this.navCtrl. push('Detail',{
    noteParam : note // key value pair
  });
}
```

To retrieve the *note* object in our detail page, add the lines shown in **bold**:

details.ts

```
import { Component } from '@angular/core';
import { IonicPage, NavController, NavParams } from 'ionic-angular';

@IonicPage()
@Component({
  selector: 'page-detail',
  templateUrl: 'detail.html',
})
export class Detail {

  note;

  constructor(public navCtrl: NavController, public navParams: NavParams)   {
    this.note = this.navParams.get('noteParam');
    console.log('nav-param',this.note);
  }

}
```

Code Explanation

Similar to *NavController*, we use an injected Ionic service called *NavParams* imported by *ionic-angular*. Our *note* object is passed in and stored in *navParams*. We retrieve the *note* object with the *get* method with the same input string '*noteParam*' used to store the parameter when we push it from home.ts.

To render our *note* title on to detail.html, add the line in **bold**:

detail.html

```
<ion-header>

  <ion-navbar>
    <ion-title>{{ note.title }}</ion-title>
  </ion-navbar>

</ion-header>

<ion-content padding>
</ion-content>
```

And you should see the title of Detail page to be the title of your note. This is how we pass parameters when navigating to another page.

Summary

In this chapter, we learnt more about working with Ionic components, listing them by iterating them in a for loop, applying pipes to values, making items clickable, how to add a new page and push it on to the navigation stack and also how to pass data between pages using the navigation parameter.

You can access the full code for this chapter at https://github.com/greglim81/ionic-chapter3and4 or contact me at support@i-ducate.com if you encounter any issues.

CHAPTER 4: BUILDING OUR NOTABLE NOTES APP (II)

We continue to build our Notable Notes app in this chapter. We will explore using additional Ionic components like ion-list, ion-items, floating action buttons, iconicons, using the scss file, implementing two-binding with Ionic fields, using the datepicker widget for date fields, implementing *service* classes to perform adding, editing, deleting of notes and more.

4.1 Editing Note Form

We want to display a form with input fields in detail.html where we are able to not just view, but edit a note.

The Ionic documentation (https://ionicframework.com/docs/components/#inputs) makes it easy for us to use Input fields. We can choose the kind of input field we want and copy and paste the code from there. In this example, I will use Fixed Inline Labels. Figure 4.1.1 shows the Ionic documentation for Fixed Inline Labels.

Fixed Inline Labels   Demo Source

Use `fixed` to place a label to the left of the input element. The label does not hide when text is entered. The input will align on the same position, regardless of the length of the label. Placeholder text can be used in conjunction with a fixed label.

```
<ion-list>

  <ion-item>
    <ion-label fixed>Username</ion-label>
    <ion-input type="text" value=""></ion-input>
  </ion-item>

  <ion-item>
    <ion-label fixed>Password</ion-label>
    <ion-input type="password"></ion-input>
  </ion-item>

</ion-list>
```

figure 4.1.1

Copy the codes from the Ionic Documentation and fill it into detail.html.

```
<ion-header>
  <ion-navbar>
    <ion-title>{{ note.title }}</ion-title>
  </ion-navbar>
</ion-header>


<ion-content padding>
  <ion-list>
    <ion-item>
      <ion-label fixed>Title</ion-label>
      <ion-input type="text" value=""></ion-input>
    </ion-item>

    <ion-item>
      <ion-label fixed>Date</ion-label>
      <ion-input type="text"></ion-input>
    </ion-item>

    <ion-item>
      <ion-textarea placeholder="Content"></ion-textarea>
    </ion-item>
  </ion-list>
</ion-content>

<ion-content padding>
```

The form contains three fields, *Title*, *Date* and *Content* wrapped in the *ion-list* component. *ion-list* is a list component used to display one or more rows of content where each row is wrapped by a *ion-item* component. Putting things in rows with *ion-list* and *ion-items* is common in mobile apps. Most items will contain an ion-label and ion-input component. These components are very similar to the standard html label and input elements. But a standard html label doesn't have certain Ionic specific attributes which gives additional animation effect to the inputs for e.g. floating labels. This is an example of extra functionality provided by Ionic components. Ionic also takes care of the styling of elements with prefix *ion* so that they look more like native mobile widgets.

Note that *Content* is placed in an *ion-textarea* which provides user to key in more content. But if we run the app now, the ion-textarea's height is only two rows. We certainly need more space to type in our notes! To increase this height, in detail.scss, add the codes in bold:

32

```
page-detail {
    textarea {
        height: 80vh;
    }
}
```

detail.scss is where we put *css* styles specific to the *detail* page. detail.scss is a *sass* file and the extra feature with *sass* compared with plain css is that we can nest selectors (we cover more about *sass* in **Appendix A: Themes**).

For example, the height specification will only apply to elements in the *page-detail* tag and class *textarea*. Ionic follows this convention where each page has a *scss* file with the same name and every rule in that file is wrapped inside *page-<pagename>* which is used to map the component selector. This way, we can isolate the styles for each page i.e. we can have another page that has *textarea* but with different style and that style won't interfere with the detail page.

So we declare the style of *textarea* to be of height *80vh*, which means to be 80 percent of the view that it is in.

Binding

Up till now, we have just a regular html form. We now want to bind each input field to the corresponding property in *note*. We will use the *[(ngModel)]* directive in Angular to implement this functionality. Add the lines below in **bold**.

```
<ion-content padding>
  <ion-list>
    <ion-item>
      <ion-label fixed>Title</ion-label>
      <ion-input type="text" [(ngModel)]="note.title" value=""></ion-input>
    </ion-item>

    <ion-item>
      <ion-label fixed>Date</ion-label>
      <ion-input type="text" [(ngModel)]="note.date"></ion-input>
    </ion-item>

    <ion-item>
      <ion-textarea placeholder="Content" [(ngModel)]="note.content"></ion-textarea>
    </ion-item>
  </ion-list>
</ion-content>
```

If we run our app now and navigate to a note, you should get something like in figure 4.1.2:

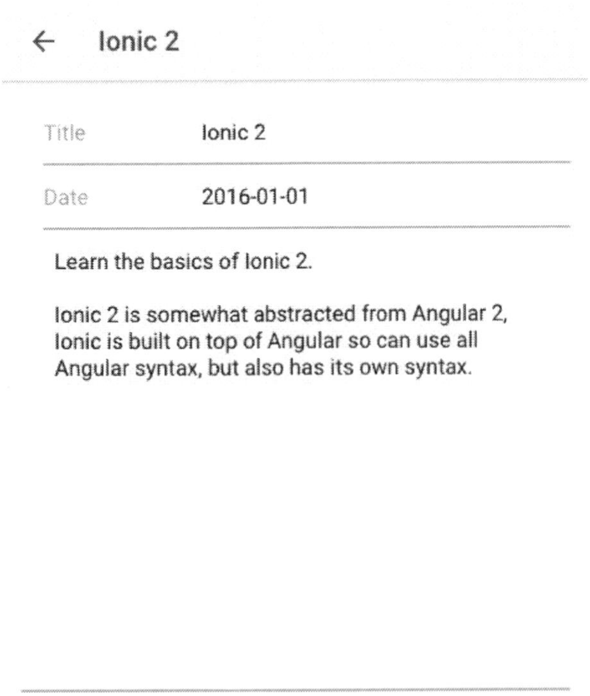

←   Ionic 2

Title	Ionic 2
Date	2016-01-01

Learn the basics of Ionic 2.

Ionic 2 is somewhat abstracted from Angular 2, Ionic is built on top of Angular so can use all Angular syntax, but also has its own syntax.

figure 4.1.2

If we modify Title, we see that the Title in the header also changes because we are doing two way binding from that input field to the property.

If we go back to the homepage, we see the changes reflected in the list. Because the note object in *detail* is 'passed by reference' from *home*, i.e. we have referenced the same *note* object in both pages.

Datetime Input

We are currently using type *text* for all the input fields. Asking a user to enter a date in YYYY-MM-DD however is not user friendly. What's more, this could introduce potential errors if a user enters YYYY-DD-MM instead. We should therefore use a datepicker widget instead.

We see in Ionic Documentation a *DateTime* component that makes it easy for users to select dates and times (fig. 4.1.3).

Buttons

Cards

Checkbox

DateTime

FABs

Gestures

Grid

DateTime

The DateTime component is used to present an interface which makes it easy for users to select dates and times. The DateTime component is similar to the native `<input type="datetime-local">` element, however, Ionic's DateTime component makes it easy to display the date and time in a preferred format, and manage the datetime values.

For more information, Check out the API docs.

figure 4.1.3

We can use this wheel picker to select the date, time, year. In detail.html, in the date input, replace *ion-input* with *ion-datetime* as shown below:

```
<ion-item>
  <ion-label fixed>Date</ion-label>
  <ion-datetime type="text" [(ngModel)]="note.date"></ion-datetime>
</ion-item>
```

35

Now when you run the app and click on the date field, it will open the date time picker for you to select.

We should in general use different field types depending on the type of data. For example, if we have a numeric input like *price*, in our input instead of *type="text"*, we should have *type="number"*. If we have a pre-defined set of options for a field like category, consider using *ion-select*.

4.2 Adding a Service

We currently define our data in *notes* array in the homepage component home.ts. As our app grows, we should keep these array data in an Angular service so that we can encapsulate it in a single class that provides all the functionality to manage *notes* data. We then inject this service into each page to share the data across components.

Create a new file in */app*, note.service.ts with the below code. Remember that an Angular service is simply a class.

```
export class NoteService{
  // copy notes data from home page
  notes = [
    {
      id: '1',
      date: '2016-01-01', //yyyy-mm-dd
      title: 'Ionic 2',
      content: 'Learn the basics of Ionic 2.'
    },
    {
      id: '2',
      date: '2016-02-01',
      title: 'Firebase',
      content: 'A great backend for Ionic applications'
    },
    {
      id: '3',
      date: '2016-03-01',
      title: 'Angular',
      content: 'A good grasp of it is crucial to developing great Ionic 2
apps.'
    }
  ];
}
```

Before we can use this service, we need to declare it in App module by adding the two lines into App Module as shown below.

```
import { NoteService } from './note.service';
...
...

  providers: [
    StatusBar,
    SplashScreen,
    NoteService,
    {provide: ErrorHandler, useClass: IonicErrorHandler}
  ]
...
```

Remember that we have to specify any application wide services we want to use in the *providers* array. In our case, we want to use the NoteService and thus add it to *providers*.

Back in home.ts, import NoteService by adding the import statement:

```
import { NoteService } from '../../app/note.service';
```

Next, inject NoteService in the *home* constructor as shown below in **bold**. We also declare a *notes* variable and assign *noteService.notes* to it.

```
export class HomePage {

  notes;

  constructor(public navCtrl: NavController, private noteService: NoteService) {
    this.notes = noteService.notes;
  }

  onItemClick(note){
    this.navCtrl. push('Detail',{
      noteParam : note
    });
  }
}
```

This will create a reference for *notes* in HomePage to the *notes* data array in *noteService*.

4.3 Deleting a Note

To implement deleting a note, first add a 'delete' button in the detail page with the code below in **bold**.

```
<ion-header>
  <ion-navbar>
    <ion-title>{{ note.title }}</ion-title>
    <ion-buttons end> <!-- // for button to be positioned right -->
      <button ion-button icon-only (click)="onTrash()">
        <ion-icon name="trash"></ion-icon>
      </button>
    </ion-buttons>
  </ion-navbar>
</ion-header>
```

We add a *ion-buttons* element with attribute *end* for the *delete* button to be positioned right. Next, we implement the *onTrash()* method in detail.ts. But before that, we implement *removeNote* in NoteService first as shown below.

```
export class NoteService{
    ...

  removeNote(note){
      let index = this.notes.indexOf(note);
      if(index > -1){
          this.notes.splice(index,1);
      }
  }
}
```

We get the index of where *note* object exists in *notes* array. If it indeed exists, i.e. index > -1, we delete it from *notes* array with the *splice* method.

Next in detail.ts, add the lines in **bold**:

```
import { Component } from '@angular/core';
import { IonicPage, NavController, NavParams } from 'ionic-angular';

import { NoteService } from '../../app/note.service';

@IonicPage()
@Component({
```

```
  selector: 'page-detail',
  templateUrl: 'detail.html',
})
export class Detail {

  note;

  constructor(public navCtrl: NavController, public navParams: NavParams,
      private noteService: NoteService) {
    this.note = this.navParams.get('noteParam');
  }

  onTrash(){
    this.noteService.removeNote(this.note);
    this.navCtrl.pop();
  }
}
```

We first import NoteService and inject an instance in the constructor. We define the *onTrash()* method and in it, call *removeNote* of *noteService*. We then pop the detail page off the stack to go back to Home page.

Ionicons

Also notice that our button is an *icon-only* button which means that it will display only an icon. This icon is defined with the *ion-icon* component inside the button element.

```
<button ion-button icon-only (click)="onTrash()">
  <ion-icon name="trash"></ion-icon>
</button>
```

In our case, we use the 'trash' icon. Ionic provides a set of beautiful icons called *Ionicons* and we can find them in the Ionic documentation under *Ionicons* (fig. 4.3.1).

Name	iOS	iOS-Outline	Material Design
add			
add-circle			
alarm			
albums			

figure 4.3.1

Notice that there are different variants for each icon: iOS, iOS-Outline and Material Design (the style used by Android). You can use the search box to find the icons you want. For example, if you search for 'folder', you get the below icons (fig. 4.3.2):

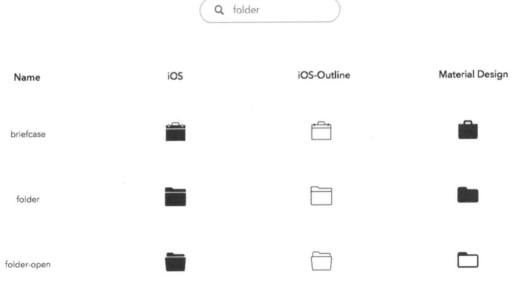

Name	iOS	iOS-Outline	Material Design
briefcase			
folder			
folder-open			

figure 4.3.2

If we click on the icon, we get a popup window (fig. 4.3.3) showing the code sample on how to use the icon. So we just need to copy the code and paste in our template.

briefcase

Usage:

```
<!--Basic: auto-select the icon based on the platform -->
<ion-icon name="briefcase"></ion-icon>

<!-- Advanced: explicity set the icon for each platform -->
<ion-icon ios="ios-briefcase" md="md-briefcase"></ion-icon>
```

figure 4.3.3

To display an icon, we use the *ion-icon* component with a name attribute where we pass in the name of the icon.

```
<ion-icon name="trash"></ion-icon>
```

Adding Alert before Deletion

Currently, a user might accidentally click on the delete icon and delete her note. To further improve our deletion so that it shows a confirmation alert before the deletion, we implement AlertController as shown below. As always, you can read more about AlertController in the Ionic Docs at https://ionicframework.com/docs/api/components/alert/AlertController/.

First in detail.ts, import *AlertController* as shown below.

```
import { IonicPage, NavController, NavParams, AlertController } from
'ionic-angular';
```

Next, inject *alertCtrl* in the constructor:

```
constructor(public navCtrl: NavController, public navParams: NavParams,
private noteService: NoteService, private alertCtrl: AlertController)
```

Finally, implement *onTrash* as shown below.

```
onTrash(){
  let confirm = this.alertCtrl.create({
    title: 'Delete?',
    message: `Are you sure you want to delete this note:
"${this.note.title}?"`, // use back tick to insert string desc
    buttons: [
      {
        text: 'Cancel' // don't do anything when cancel
      },
      {
        text: 'Confirm',
        handler: () => {
          this.noteService.removeNote(this.note);
          this.navCtrl.pop();
        }
      }
    ]
  });
  confirm.present();
}
```

Code Explanation

The above code creates an Alert Controller *alertCtrl* with the title, message and two buttons 'Cancel', 'Confirm' (as defined in *buttons* array). We also do something if user clicks on 'Confirm', which is call *removeNote* method of *noteService* and then proceed to pop *detail* page off the navigation stack.

4.4 Adding a New Note

To add a new note, we will use the Floating Action Button or FAB. FABs are buttons styled after Google's specification. It's the round icon button that floats on the page. An example is the 'Compose Mail' button in the Gmail app (figure 4.4.1). An FAB always stays in the same position even though scrolling takes place.

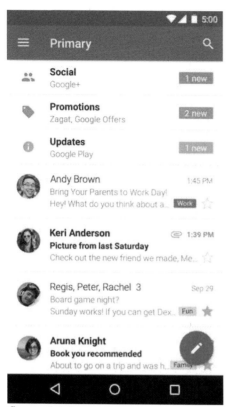

figure 4.4.1

Ionic provides its own FAB component via the *ion-fab* attribute.

To add a 'add' FAB in our home page, add the following codes in **bold** in home.html:

```
<ion-content padding>
  <ion-card *ngFor="let note of notes" (click)="onItemClick(note)"> <!--
ion-item -->
    <ion-card-header>
      {{ note.date | date }}
    </ion-card-header>
    <ion-card-content>
      <ion-card-title>
        {{ note.title }}
      </ion-card-title>
      <p>
        {{ note.content }}
      </p>
```

```
      </ion-card-content>
    </ion-card>
    <ion-fab right bottom>
      <button ion-fab color="primary" (click)="onAddClick()">
        <ion-icon name="add"></ion-icon>
      </button>
    </ion-fab>
</ion-content>
```

With the *right bottom* attribute, we choose to display the FAB in the bottom right. We can also choose to position else where like top right, left bottom etc. Also note that the FAB button always stays in the same position whether you scroll or resize the screen. Let's now implement the *onAddClick()* method by adding the following method in home.ts.

```
onAddClick(){
   this.navCtrl.push('Detail'); // for add, don't pass in any parameters.
}
```

The onAddClick method simply pushes the detail page onto the navigation stack without any *note* object as parameter. This however causes an error to be thrown when the app tries to show the detail page because *note* is empty. To correct this, add the codes in **bold** in detail.ts.

```
export class Detail {

  note;
  newNoteFlag = false;

  constructor(public navCtrl: NavController, public navParams: NavParams,
private noteService: NoteService, private alertCtrl: AlertController) {
    this.note = this.navParams.get('noteParam');

    if(!this.note){
      this.note = {
        id: '',
        date: '',
        title: '',
        content: ''
      };
      this.newNoteFlag = true;
    }
  }
}
```

So now, we check if *note* object is null which means that it was not sent in by *navParams* meaning that it came from an *add* instead of an *edit* operation. If its null, we then set note to an

44

empty object which then allows the detail page to be rendered with all the fields as empty. We also set *newNoteFlag* to *true* indicating that this note is a new note. This will allow us to later differentiate if its a new note or an existing note when we go back to the home page

Next, implement *addNote* in NoteService with the below codes in **bold**.

```
export class NoteService{
    ...
  addNote(note) {
    this.notes.push(note);
  }
}
```

We then call *addNote* when the user clicks on the back button. To handle the event when a user clicks on the back button, we implement the *ionViewWillLeave* event. The *ionViewWillLeave* event is called when the page is about to leave and no longer be the active page.

In detail.ts, implement the *ionViewWillLeave* method as shown below.

```
  ionViewWillLeave() {

    if(this.note.title=== "" && this.note.date=== "" && this.note.content=== ""){
      // if note is blank don't do anything
    }
    else if(this.newNoteFlag){
      this.noteService.addNote(this.note);
    }
    else{
      // editing note. do nothing
    }
  }
```

Notice that when we are about to leave *detail* page, we check for the note's fields if they are just an empty string, and if so, we don't do anything. This will prevent us from adding multiple blank notes.

If the note is not empty and the *newNoteFlag* is true, we proceed to add the note.

Lastly, we want to show the delete button only for editing note and hide it when we are adding a new note. To do so, we can use the *newNoteFlag* in detail.html as shown below.

```
<button ion-button icon-only (click)="onTrash()" *ngIf="!newNoteFlag" >
    <!-- show trash button only if its existing note -->
```

45

Summary

We implemented editing, deleting and adding of notes with forms consisting of Ionic labels, input fields, date-time picker widgets, ionicons and alerts. We also created a service class to encapsulate the code needed to support these functionalities.

At this point, our app is almost done. The drawback is of course that our data is stored only in memory and not persistent i.e. all data is gone when the app restarts. We will implement data persistency in a later chapter. But for now, we will see how to deploy our app to an actual device.

You can access the full code for this chapter at https://github.com/greglim81/ionic-chapter3and4

CHAPTER 5: DEPLOYING TO A DEVICE

Many Ionic native plugins will only work when they are ran on an actual advice. To accurately test how our app will behave and perform, we will learn how to deploy on an actual device in this chapter. This will later allow us to upload our app on to the Apple App Store or Google Play Store.

5.1 Requirements for Deploying to Android Devices

We will first need the latest version of Android Studio and the Android SDK which is available through the Android Studio's SDK Manager. Install the latest version of Android Studio.

Next, we will need to enable 'Developer Mode' on our Android device. Since each Android device's user interface can vary, these are the general instructions:

- navigating to 'Settings' > 'About Phone'
- scroll to the bottom where there should be a build number. Tap it seven times.
- Once that is done, there should be a short pop-up in the lower area of your display saying that you're now a developer.
- If we go back to the Settings list, we should see a new Developer Options item.
- Enable 'USB debugging' by accessing the Developer options menu, check 'USB debugging' and click OK on the prompt. Our Android device is now ready for development.

If you face problems, the exact steps differ according to different Android phone models. So, a quick Google search will let you know the exact steps to enable 'Developer Mode and USD debugging'.

Adding Mobile Platforms

In Cordova terminology, Android and iOS are platforms. The Ionic CLI includes a platform command that we use to manage the Cordova platforms in our project. So the first step we need before we can build a project for a certain platform is to add that platform to our project. We do that in the command line by typing:

ionic cordova platform add <platform name>

Run *ionic cordova platform add android* to first add the Android platform to your project.

This will download various packages required to build the app for Android. The generated platform specific files are kept in the *platforms* folder and there is now a sub folder for Android. We don't have to worry exactly what the files are because Cordova takes care of it for us. But if you are familiar with Android development, you will see familiar files like AndroidManifest.xml. Note that we only need to add the Android platform once.

The command to add iOS platform to our project is *ionic cordova platform add ios*. By default, the iOS platform is added if you are running on a Mac.

Building for Android

Next, we will run the command to build our app for Android.

ionic cordova build

The Terminal will prompt you to select the platform you would like to build in. Choose Android.

Ionic will build our project as a web app to start with, and later package the web app inside a native Android app. This creates an *apk* file that is an Android app package. An *apk* file is basically a zip file that contains compiled Java code and in our case also static web files like html, css, js, images, fonts and so on. Our Android app will display a native web view component that will load our index.html page which will in turn load our js code, css styles and so on and run our app as a web page.

Note by default that the *ionic cordova build* command creates a debug build which we want for testing but we cannot use this to publish it on Google Play. To publish on Google Play, we will later need to create a release build for that. To create a build for publish, we run:

ionic build android --prod

The *--prod* option enables Javascript optimizations when building the web app. In addition, to deploy on Google Play, we also need to add the *--release* option to create a release build. We will cover this later in **Chapter 11 – Deploying to the App Store**. But we will not enable the *--release* option for now as we want to enable our app for testing first in the Android emulator.

Running on Android Emulator

After adding the Android platform to our project, we can choose to run our app in the emulator or in a real device. The emulator has the advantage that you can use it to test different Android versions or if you do not have a real Android phone available. We will illustrate running our app on the emulator. Start the emulator first by typing:

```
android avd
```

This will open the Android Virtual Device (AVD) manager. The launcher takes a while to boot (about 30 over seconds) and that is why we launch the emulator first before we run the *ionic cordova emulate* command. If you do not have the emulator launched before hand, the *ionic cordova emulate* command will also launch the emulator. But because of the long time taken by the emulator launching, the Ionic command sometimes times-out and does not work properly. So it's more reliable if you have the emulator already running.

In the AVD manager, you can select the device configuration you want in the Device Definitions tab. Select a definition and click the 'Create AVD' button. This will open a new window with configurations that you set for your virtual device like screen size, Android version to run, etc. Click OK to finish the process once you are done. You can have as many virtual devices as you want.

Once the emulator is running, in your project folder in the terminal, type

ionic cordova emulate android --prod

The *--prod* creates a production build of our webapp. A production build loads and runs faster in Android although it takes longer to build. Note that the *ionic cordova emulate* command does a new build of our project every time so there is no need to run *ionic cordova build* before, it does that automatically.

Our app should now run in the emulator. (We will look at changing the names and icon of our app in config.xml later.)

Running on an Android Device

Now let's see how to run our app in a real device. It's similar to running it in the emulator. The difference is that instead of *ionic cordova emulate*, the command is *ionic cordova run*. Now to run your app in a device, you need to connect your Android phone to your computer.

You can check from your computer to see if your device is properly connected by typing

adb devices

adb stands for android debug bridge and it's the part of the Android SDK used to communicate with the Android system. You should see your device listed there. When your device is properly connected, run:

ionic cordova run android

After a while (it takes longer because it's a 'dev' build), you can see your app running on the Android phone.

Developing/Debugging on Android

Now what if your app doesn't work properly for whatever reason? How can we debug it? We can debug our app while it's running on Android just like a regular web app thanks to Chrome remote debugging feature.

Open a new chrome tab and type:

chrome://inspect

chrome is a special protocol used to access internal browser tools and *inspect* looks for any webpage that can be debugged.

It finds a remote target called *Android SDK built for x86* which is the name of the system running on the emulator and on that target, it detected a webview that runs our app. If we click *inspect*, it will open the Chrome developer tools for debugging that web page. The dev tools even mirrors the rendered page. Thanks to the remote debugging feature, we have the full power of Chrome developer tools available to inspect our app running in a webview on Android including looking at the console for any log messages.

We can also use the dev tools to inspect any element on the page and see details about their styles. For e.g. show the css styles used by a field. This is useful not just to investigate problems in our code through the console but also to debug styling issues. We can pretty much use all of the developer tools.

Livereload

It is painful whenever we make a code change and have to wait two minutes to wait for ionic emulate, ionic run and wait for the app to build and install. So, it is nice if we can refresh the app automatically at every change like when we run it in the browser with the *ionic serve* command. That is the usefulness of Chrome remote debugging which provides live reloading of the app which we cannot easily do in Android Studio.

If we type *ionic help cordova emulate*, we see all the options, and one of the options is *--livereload* 'Live reload app dev files from the device'. That is, we can run:

```
ionic cordova emulate android --livereload
```

or with a real device

```
ionic cordova run android --livereload
```

Now if you try changing something in your code, it will detect that a file is modified and reload our app. So live reload works on Android making it very convenient and productive for app development.

5.2 Requirements for Deploying to iOS Devices

To compile and package iOS apps, you first need to install Xcode 7 or higher which only runs on MacOS. I recommend you install the latest version of Xcode from the Mac App Store.

You will need a iOS device running on at least iOS9. As of iOS9, you can develop and test apps on your iOS device without a paid Apple Developer account. This is great if you want to try out development with Ionic and do not yet have a paid Apple developer account.

Creating a Provisioning Profile

To start, we will need a provisioning profile to code sign our apps for testing.

Using an Apple ID

To create a provisioning profile using an Apple ID (if you don't have a paid Apple developer account), do the following steps:

- Open Xcode preferences (Xcode > Preferences…)
- Click the 'Accounts' tab
- Login with your Apple ID

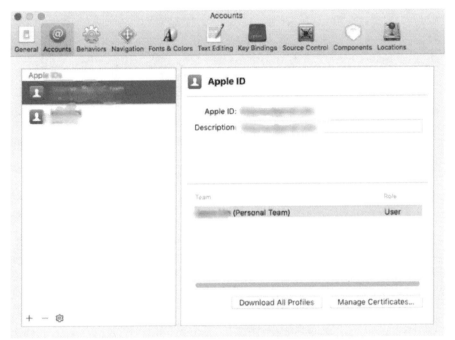

figure 5.2.1

When you have successfully logged in, a new 'Personal Team' will appear (fig. 5.2.1).

Using an Apple Developer Account

There are certain additional steps to create a provisioning profile with a paid Apple Developer account. Do the following:

- Run a production build of your app by typing the following command in the Terminal *ionic cordova build ios --prod*
- Open the *.xcodeproj* file in */platforms/ios/* of your project folder in Xcode.
- Connect your iOS device via USB and select it as the run target.
- Click the play button in Xcode to try to run your app.

At this point, you will encounter a code signing error something like:

Signing for <projectname> requires a development team. Select a development team in the project. Code signing is required for product type 'Application' in SDK...

Code Signing Our App

We will need to select the certificate to code sign our app. This is Apple's security feature to make sure that each app can be traced back to a specific developer. Do the following:

- Click on the your project name in the 'Project Navigator' to go to the Project Editor
- Select 'General'
- Select the team associate from the 'Team' dropdown in the 'Signing' section.

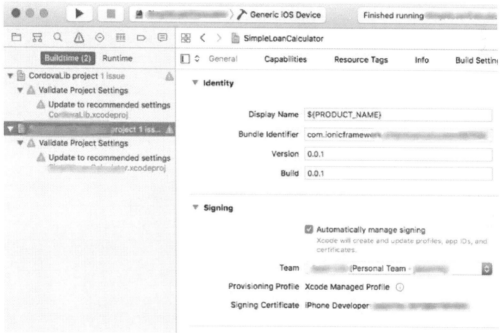

figure 5.2.2

Trusting the Certificate

Once we have code signed our app, we will get a launch error like

Could not launch "testApp"

Verify the Developer App certificate for your account is trusted on your device. Open Settings on Alex's iPhone and navigate to General -> Device Management, then select your Developer App certificate to trust it.

OK

To resolve this, we need to tell our iOS device to trust the certificate we code signed our app with. This is a security measure to stop people from accidentally installing apps from outside the App store that may contain viruses. iOS will refuse to install any app unless we explicitly declare that we trust this developer. On your iOS device, do the following:

From your device, as the message says, open *Settings, General, Device Management,* click on developer id, and we can see what apps we installed from this developer. Click *Trust* and *Confirm.* Running our app on a device should work now.

You should now be able to run your app on the iOS device. Go back to Xcode and click 'Play' to launch your app.

We met some complexity when developing for iOS because each app has to be signed with a developer certificate for security reasons. The simplest approach is to let Xcode manage signing automatically and that is why the first time we build our project, we open our project in Xcode.

Running on iOS from the Command Line

The first time we tried running the *ionic build ios* command, we got an error because we were missing a signing certificate. But after we opened the project in Xcode, we configured a developer account and enabled automatic signing. After these setups, we should be able to run our app on a device from the command line by running *ionic cordova build iOS (ionic cordova build iOS* creates an *iOS.app* file in the build folder).

Running on the Emulator

Similar to the build process for Android, *ionic cordova emulate ios* builds our project as a webapp and then compiles in into iOS code to run the app in the simulator. (Note the terminology used, in Android, its an emulator and in iOS, its simulator). When the simulator is ready, it will launch our app.

54

With Android, we can use Chrome remote debugging to attach developer tools to our app. We can do a similar thing to iOS by using Safari instead of Chrome. In Safari menu, go to -> Develop -> Simulator -> NotableNotes. This opens the Safari web inspector and we can do the same things we did with Chrome developer tools like inspect html elements and css styles.

Livereload

We can also run our app with the *livereload* option as shown below.

```
ionic cordova emulate ios --livereload
```

With the *livereload* option, any code changes will automatically be reflected in the iOS app. So whatever we did for Android we can do for iOS as well.

Running on the Device

If you have a iOS device connected by USB, you can launch your app by typing

```
ionic cordova run ios
```

Like for Android, you can also pass in option *--prod* to enable Javascript code optimization.

Note that you can also prefer to launch your app from Xcode but in that case, the live reload functionality will not be available.

5.3 Configuring App Icon, Splash Screen Images

To configure app icons, images, names and other app metadata, we edit the config.xml file in the root directory.

For example, the below in config.xml shows the configuration for different icons with different screen densities for an Android app:

```
<platform name="android">
    <!--
        ldpi     : 36x36 px
        mdpi     : 48x48 px
        hdpi     : 72x72 px
        xhdpi    : 96x96 px
        xxhdpi   : 144x144 px
```

```
        xxxhdpi : 192x192 px
    -->
    <icon src="res/android/ldpi.png" density="ldpi" />
    <icon src="res/android/mdpi.png" density="mdpi" />
    <icon src="res/android/hdpi.png" density="hdpi" />
    <icon src="res/android/xhdpi.png" density="xhdpi" />
    <icon src="res/android/xxhdpi.png" density="xxhdpi" />
    <icon src="res/android/xxxhdpi.png" density="xxxhdpi" />
</platform>
```

If your phone has a lower resolution, Android will use a smaller icon. Devices with larger resolution, will use a larger icon.

iOS takes a similar approach. Instead of *density*, it uses *width* and *height* attributes as shown below.

```
<platform name="ios">
    <!-- iOS 8.0+ -->
    <!-- iPhone 6 Plus   -->
    <icon src="res/ios/icon-60@3x.png" width="180" height="180" />
    <!-- iOS 7.0+ -->
    <!-- iPhone / iPod Touch  -->
    <icon src="res/ios/icon-60.png" width="60" height="60" />
    <icon src="res/ios/icon-60@2x.png" width="120" height="120" />
    <!-- iPad -->
    <icon src="res/ios/icon-76.png" width="76" height="76" />
    <icon src="res/ios/icon-76@2x.png" width="152" height="152" />
    <!-- Spotlight Icon -->
    <icon src="res/ios/icon-40.png" width="40" height="40" />
    <icon src="res/ios/icon-40@2x.png" width="80" height="80" />
    <!-- iOS 6.1 -->
    <!-- iPhone / iPod Touch -->
    <icon src="res/ios/icon.png" width="57" height="57" />
    <icon src="res/ios/icon@2x.png" width="114" height="114" />
    <!-- iPad -->
    <icon src="res/ios/icon-72.png" width="72" height="72" />
    <icon src="res/ios/icon-72@2x.png" width="144" height="144" />
    <!-- iPhone Spotlight and Settings Icon -->
    <icon src="res/ios/icon-small.png" width="29" height="29" />
    <icon src="res/ios/icon-small@2x.png" width="58" height="58" />
    <!-- iPad Spotlight and Settings Icon -->
    <icon src="res/ios/icon-50.png" width="50" height="50" />
    <icon src="res/ios/icon-50@2x.png" width="100" height="100" />
    <!-- iPad Pro -->
    <icon src="res/ios/icon-83.5@2x.png" width="167" height="167" />
</platform>
```

Note that the above configurations is just for the app icon. We also need different images for the splash screen. To create different images sizes for the app icon and splash screen would consume a lot of time! Thankfully, Ionic makes our lives easier.

Ionic CLI includes a command that can generate all the required images automatically! The *ionic help resources* command tells us:

"Automatically create icon and splash screen resources (beta)
Put your images in the ./resources directory, named splash or icon.
Accepted file types are .png, .ai, and .psd.
Icons should be 192x192 px without rounded corners.
Splash screens should be 2208x2208 px, with the image centered in the middle."

The message in *help* refer to a folder called *resources* which store icon.png and splash.png.

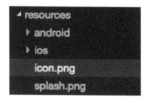

So to have your own icon and splash screen, in *resources*, replace icon.png and splash.png with your own icon and splash screen image file. For the best results, your icon file should be 1,024 by 1,024 pixels in size. You should also not include any platform-specific effects like round corners and glossy overlays. When your icon image is ready, name it *icon.png*

Your splash screen file should be at least 2,208 by 2,208 pixels in size. Splash screens should be rectangular and can be oriented in both portrait and landscape mode. If your application runs only in a particular orientation, you need only to supply the splash screen for that orientation. When your splash screen image is ready, name it *splash.png*.

When both icon.png and splash.png are done, use the *ionic resources* command to generate for all the various sizes for Android and iOS. Note that the CLI will also accept Photoshop (PSD) files but we recommend sticking with *png* file as the source.

If you look at the *resources* folder again, you will see the various image sizes generated. And also in config.xml (example below), *ionic resources* has added all the required configuration in it.

```xml
<platform name="ios">
  <allow-intent href="itms:*"/>
  <allow-intent href="itms-apps:*"/>
  <icon src="resources/ios/icon/icon.png" width="57" height="57"/>
  <icon src="resources/ios/icon/icon@2x.png" width="114" height="114"/>
  <icon src="resources/ios/icon/icon-40.png" width="40" height="40"/>
  <icon src="resources/ios/icon/icon-40@2x.png" width="80" height="80"/>
  <icon src="resources/ios/icon/icon-40@3x.png" width="120" height="120"/>
  <icon src="resources/ios/icon/icon-50.png" width="50" height="50"/>
  <icon src="resources/ios/icon/icon-50@2x.png" width="100" height="100"/>
  <icon src="resources/ios/icon/icon-60.png" width="60" height="60"/>
  <icon src="resources/ios/icon/icon-60@2x.png" width="120" height="120"/>
  <icon src="resources/ios/icon/icon-60@3x.png" width="180" height="180"/>
  <icon src="resources/ios/icon/icon-72.png" width="72" height="72"/>
  <icon src="resources/ios/icon/icon-72@2x.png" width="144" height="144"/>
  <icon src="resources/ios/icon/icon-76.png" width="76" height="76"/>
  <icon src="resources/ios/icon/icon-76@2x.png" width="152" height="152"/>
  <icon src="resources/ios/icon/icon-83.5@2x.png" width="167" height="167"/>
  <icon src="resources/ios/icon/icon-small.png" width="29" height="29"/>
  <icon src="resources/ios/icon/icon-small@2x.png" width="58" height="58"/>
  <icon src="resources/ios/icon/icon-small@3x.png" width="87" height="87"/>
  <splash src="resources/ios/splash/Default-568h@2x~iphone.png" width="640" height="1136"/>
  <splash src="resources/ios/splash/Default-667h.png" width="750" height="1334"/>
  <splash src="resources/ios/splash/Default-736h.png" width="1242" height="2208"/>
  <splash src="resources/ios/splash/Default-Landscape~ipad.png" width="1024" height="768"/>

  <splash src="resources/ios/splash/Default-Portrait~ipad.png" width="768" height="1024"/>
  <splash src="resources/ios/splash/Default@2x~iphone.png" width="640" height="960"/>
  <splash src="resources/ios/splash/Default~iphone.png" width="320" height="480"/>
</platform>
```

This saves us a lot of boring work. If we run our app now in the Android emulator and in the iOS simulator, the app icon and splash icons should reflect the updated ones.

5.4 Configuring Other App Metadata

The below sections list other elements of config.xml that you will need to update for your application.

App id and version

```xml
<widget id="com.ionicframework.notablenotes102230" version="0.0.1"
```

id is the unique identifier for our application. You should later supply your own *id* when you publish and sign your application. The *id* should be in reverse-domain name style, e.g. com.yourcompany.yourapp.

We can change the version number that we want to display in the App store, for example `version="1.0.0"`. We should increment the version number with each new release.

App name and description

```
<name>NotableNotes</name>
<description>An awesome Ionic/Cordova app.</description>
```

We can specify the name and description of the app.

Author email, website and display name

```
<author email="hi@ionicframework" href="http://ionicframework.com/">Ionic
Framework Team</author>
```

We specify the author email, webpage and name to be displayed. All these will be displayed in the App store.

The above information are the basic info that you need for your app and should be sufficient. If you need more specific information about config.xml, you can refer to the official Cordova at https://cordova.apache.org/docs/en/latest/config_ref/.

Try it Out

After editing config.xml, if you build and run your app, the changes will be reflected in the device.

Summary

We learnt how to build and deploy our projects to the Android/iOS emulator and device. With *livereload*, we learnt how to debug while our app is deployed in the emulator or device. We also covered how to configure app metadata as well as generate the needed image resources.

CHAPTER 6: STORING DATA

Our NotableNotes app from chapter four has a drawback in that data is stored only in memory and therefore not persistent. In this chapter, we will implement data persistency using the *Storage* library provided in Ionic.

6.1 Using Storage to Set and Get Data

Ionic provides the *Storage* library to enable us to persistently store our data in our device. *Storage* automatically runs a fitting way of storage depending on the device we are running our Ionic code on. When running on a native app, it will try to prioritize SQLite which is a little database running on our device by default. If on a browser, it will use IndexedDB, WebSQL and LocalStorage in that order. But all these are behind the scenes and we do not have to worry about these details.

Using Storage is fairly straightforward. First, install the cordova-sqlite-storage plugin:

```
ionic cordova plugin add cordova-sqlite-storage –save
```

The package is already included in our node modules, so we only need to import it in our *imports* array of App Module.

app.module.ts

We first import *IonicStorageModule* in App Module as shown below.

```
...

import { NoteService } from './note.service';
import { IonicStorageModule } from '@ionic/storage';

@NgModule({
  declarations: [
    MyApp,
    HomePage
  ],
  imports: [
    BrowserModule,
    IonicModule.forRoot(MyApp),
    IonicStorageModule.forRoot()
  ],
```

```
bootstrap: [IonicApp],
...
```

note.service.ts

Storage will only be used in NoteService where we hide the implementation details from home and detail page. We access *Storage* whenever we fetch, add, edit or delete a note. In note.service.ts, add the lines in bold as shown:

```
import { Storage } from '@ionic/storage';
import { Injectable } from '@angular/core';

@Injectable()
export class NoteService{

  // copy notes data from home page
  notes;

  constructor(private storage : Storage){
  }

  fetchNotes(){
    return this.storage.get('notes')
      .then(
        (notes) => {
          notes? this.notes = notes : this.notes = [];
      })
      .catch(
        err => console.log(err)
      );
  }

  removeNote(note){
      let index = this.notes.indexOf(note);
      if(index > -1){
        this.notes.splice(index,1);
        this.writeToStorage();
      }
  }

  addNote(note){
    this.notes.push(note);
    this.writeToStorage();
  }

  editNote(note){
```

```
      this.writeToStorage();
  }

  writeToStorage(){
    this.storage.set('notes',this.notes) // set key-value pairs
    .then(// successful add
    // do nothing
    )
    .catch(err => {// catch errors and do error handling here
        err => console.log(err);
    });
  }
}
```

Code Explanation

```
import { Storage } from '@ionic/storage';
import { Injectable } from '@angular/core';

@Injectable()
```

We first import *Storage* and *Injectable*. We need to add the *@Injectable()* decorator before the service class because *@Injectable()* marks a class as available for dependency injection. You might be asking, but didn't we so far omit *@Injectable()* from NoteService? This was possible because NoteService previously had no injected parameters, i.e. its constructor was blank. But we must have it now because the service has an injected dependency *Storage* in the constructor as shown below.

```
  constructor(private storage : Storage){
  }
```

In general, add *@Injectable()* to every service class, even those that don't have dependencies so you don't have to remember *@Injectable()* when you add a dependency later. This also makes it consistent for all services.

fetchNotes()

```
fetchNotes(){
    return this.storage.get('notes')
      .then(
        (notes) => {
          notes? this.notes = notes : this.notes = [];
        })
```

63

```
      .catch(
        err => console.log(err)
      );
  }
```

We then have the *fetchNotes()* method which calls *storage.get()*. Because *Storage* stores its objects in a key/value pair format, we store our *notes* array as value with the key 'notes'. To retrieve it we call the *get()* method and supply it with 'notes' as key. *storage.get()* returns a Promise with the value of the given key. Using *then*, we retrieve the value.

```
notes? this.notes = notes : this.notes = [];
```

With the above line, we assign to *notes* only if the value returned is not null. If the value returned is null, especially when the app first starts, we instantiate notes to an empty array.

writeToStorage()

```
  writeToStorage(){
    this.storage.set('notes',this.notes) // set key-value pairs
    .then(// successful add
    // do nothing
    )
    .catch(err => {// catch errors and do error handling here
        err => console.log(err);
    });
  }
```

writeToStorage() as its name suggest simply writes to *Storage*. In it, with storage.*set()*, we set *notes* array with the key 'notes' for methods like *fetchNotes()* to later retrieve it. Similar to *get()*, *set()* returns a returns a Promise that resolves when the key and value are set.

addNote() and *removeNote()*

Having implemented *writeToStorage()*, we then proceed to use it in *addNote()* and *removeNote()* as shown below:

```
  removeNote(note){
      let index = this.notes.indexOf(note);
      if(index > -1){
        this.notes.splice(index,1);
        this.writeToStorage();
      }
  }
```

64

```
addNote(note){
  this.notes.push(note);
  this.writeToStorage();
}
```

The *remove* and *add* note methods remain similar as before, except that we call *writeToStorage* at the end.

6.2 Calling NoteService

Having implemented *Storage* in NoteService, we can now call it from *detail* and *home* page. The changes to *detail* and *home* are minimal since we have largely encapsulated implementation details in NoteService. But there are some places where we still have to make a few changes.

detail.ts

In detail.ts, make the codes as shown in **bold**:

```
...
export class Detail {

  note;
  newNoteFlag = false;
  deleteNoteFlag = false;

  constructor(...
    ...
  }

  onTrash(){
    let confirm = this.alertCtrl.create({
      title: 'Delete?',
      message: `Are you sure you want to delete this note: "${this.note.title}?"`,
// use back tick to insert string desc
      buttons: [
        {
          text: 'Cancel' // don't do anything when cancel
        },
        {
          text: 'Confirm',
          handler: () => {
            //this.noteService.removeNote(this.note);
            this.deleteNoteFlag = true;
            this.navCtrl.pop();
          }
        }
```

```
    ]
  });
  confirm.present();
}

ionViewWillLeave() {

  if(this.note.title=== "" && this.note.date=== "" && this.note.content=== ""){
    // if note is blank don't do anything
  }
  else if(this.newNoteFlag){
    this.noteService.addNote(this.note);
    console.log("add note");
  }
  else if(this.deleteNoteFlag){
    this.noteService.removeNote(this.note);
    console.log("delete note");
  }
  else{
    this.noteService.writeToStorage();
    console.log("edit note");
  }
}
}
```

Code Explanation

To make our code cleaner and avoid writing to persistent disk space storage twice, we move our *deleteNote()* call to in *ionViewWillLeave()*. We define *deleteNoteFlag* which is set to true in *onTrash()*. And if user clicks on the delete button, *deleteNoteFlag* is set to true and *NoteService removeNote()* will be called when user goes back to the home page.

In the case of editing a note, code execution will be brought to the last *else* clause which will keep the changes persistent by calling *noteService.writeToStorage()* before returning to the home page.

fetchNotes()

home.ts

Next in home.ts, we implement the *ngOnInit* method and call the *fetchNotes()* method of *noteService* in it. If you are asking why not call *fetchNotes* in the constructor? A constructor is meant only for light weight operations and for heavier operations like fetching data from a service, we should implement them in *ngOnInit*.

```
export class HomePage {

  notes;

  constructor(public    navCtrl:    NavController,    private    noteService:
NoteService) {
  }

  ngOnInit(){
    this.noteService.fetchNotes()
      .then(res => {
        this.notes = this.noteService.notes;
      });
  }
}
```

Note that since *fetchNotes()* return a Promise, we should receive the returned *notes* array in the *then* block.

Running Your App

With that, implementing data persistency with Storage is completed. Try running your app now and when re-loading it, you will find that your data is preserved.

Summary

We learnt how to use the Ionic Storage library to store data persistently in the device. You can access the full code for this chapter at https://github.com/greglim81/ionic-chapter6

In the next chapter, we look at how to store data on a remote server using Firebase.

CHAPTER 7: C.R.U.D. WITH FIREBASE

In this chapter, we look at storing data remotely on Firebase. We will see how to make requests to communicate with Firebase to implement full C.R.U.D. operations. A typical mobile application architecture consists of the server side and client side. In this book, we implement the client side using Ionic. In a normal mobile app client server architecture, the client side talks to the backend server to get or save data typically via RESTful http services built using service side frameworks like ASP.NET, Node.js and Ruby on Rails. Building the server side however is often time consuming and not in the scope of this book. In this chapter, we circumvent the difficulties of implementing the server side by using Firebase as our backend server.

Firebase is a service from Google which gives you a ready to use backend. You don't have to write any server side code to get database, authentication, storage features and much more. These allow us to focus on building our application according to requirements rather than debugging server side code.

The main feature we will use in this chapter is the real-time, fast and scalable NoSQL cloud database provided by firebase. Firebase provides a library for us to talk to the database in Typescript. A NoSQL database consists of a tree of JSON objects where each node in the tree can have a different structure. This is in contrast to a relational database which consist of tables and relationships. An advantage of this is that we don't have to worry about maintaining table schemas and therefore increase productivity. However, if your application involves lots of data aggregating, complex querying and reporting, a relational database might still be a better choice.

The aim of this chapter is to illustrate create, read, update and delete functionality with Ionic and Firebase so that you can go on and create a fully working app. And in the next two chapters, we will focus on using Firebase to authenticate and authorize users who use our app.

7.1 Using Firebase

We can use Firebase features for free and only pay when our application grows bigger. You can choose between a subscription based or 'pay as you use' model. Find out more at firebase.google.com/pricing.

Before adding Firebase to our Ionic project, we need to first create a Firebase account. Go to firebase.google.com and sign in with your Google account.

Click **'Get Started for Free'** to go to the Firebase console. In the console, click on 'Create New Project' (figure 12.1)

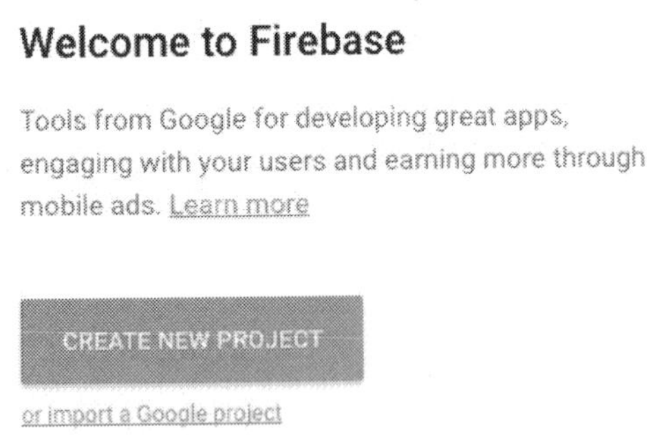

Welcome to Firebase

Tools from Google for developing great apps, engaging with your users and earning more through mobile ads. Learn more

CREATE NEW PROJECT

or import a Google project

figure 7.1.1

Fill in the project name, country and click 'Create Project'.

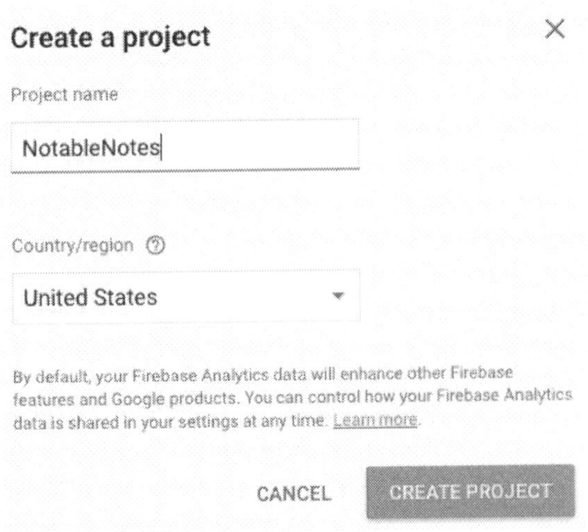

Create a project   ✕

Project name

NotableNotes

Country/region ⑦

United States ▾

By default, your Firebase Analytics data will enhance other Firebase features and Google products. You can control how your Firebase Analytics data is shared in your settings at any time. Learn more.

CANCEL   CREATE PROJECT

figure 7.1.2

In the Welcome screen, click on 'Add Firebase to your web app' (figure 7.1.3).

Welcome to Firebase! Get started here.

Add Firebase to your iOS app   **Add Firebase to your Android app**   **Add Firebase to your web app**

figure 7.1.3

You will see some configuration code that you need to add in your project (fig. 7.1.4).

Add Firebase to your web app   ✕

Copy and paste the snippet below at the bottom of your HTML, before other `script` tags.

```
<script src="https://www.gstatic.com/firebasejs/3.9.0/firebase.js"></script>
<script>
  // Initialize Firebase
  var config = {
    apiKey: "AIzaSyAonCRyv2DeV75eHxU3GunvbuNpbYqprAY",
    authDomain: "notablenotes-82b3d.firebaseapp.com",
    databaseURL: "https://notablenotes-82b3d.firebaseio.com",
    projectId: "notablenotes-82b3d",
    storageBucket: "notablenotes-82b3d.appspot.com",
    messagingSenderId: "1010273852261"
  };
  firebase.initializeApp(config);
</script>
```

COPY

figure 7.1.4

Code Explanation

```
<script src="https://www.gstatic.com/firebasejs/3.9.0/firebase.js"></script>
```

This is a script reference to Firebase SDK. firebase.js gives us a library to work with firebase.

```
<script>
  // Initialize Firebase
  var config = {
```

71

```
    apiKey: "AIzaSyAonCRyv2DeV75eHxU3GunvbuNpbYqprAY",
    authDomain: "notablenotes-82b3d.firebaseapp.com",
    databaseURL: "https://notablenotes-82b3d.firebaseio.com",
    projectId: "notablenotes-82b3d",
    storageBucket: "notablenotes-82b3d.appspot.com",
    messagingSenderId: "1010273852261"
  };
  firebase.initializeApp(config);
</script>
```

We have a *config* or configuration object with properties *apiKey*, *authDomain* (a subdomain under firebaseapp.com), *databaseUrl*, *storageBucket* (for storing files like photos, videos etc.) and *messagingSenderId* (used for sending push notifications).

7.2 Adding Firebase to our Ionic App

Next, use *npm* to add firebase and another library called *angularfire* to our project.

```
npm install firebase angularfire2 --save
```

After the installation, an entry in package.json for firebase will have been added (see lines below in **bold**).

```
  "dependencies": {
    ...
    "@angular/platform-browser": "4.0.2",
    "@angular/platform-browser-dynamic": "4.0.2",
    "@ionic-native/core": "3.6.1",
    "@ionic-native/splash-screen": "3.6.1",
    "@ionic-native/status-bar": "3.6.1",
    "@ionic/storage": "^2.0.1",
    "angularfire2": "^4.0.0-rc.0",
    "firebase": "^3.9.0",
    "ionic-angular": "3.1.1",
    "ionicons": "3.0.0",
    "rxjs": "5.1.1",
    "sw-toolbox": "3.4.0",
    "uuid": "^3.0.1",
    "zone.js": "^0.8.10"
  },
```

(Note: At time of writing, the version for "angularfire2": "^4.0.0-rc.0", and "firebase":

72

```
"^3.9.0")
```

app.module.ts

As of AngularFire2 4.0.0, we need to import *AngularFireModule* and also *AngularFireDatabaseModule* into app.module.ts (if you are using firebase version before 4.0.0, you need to import only *AngularFireModule*). In app.module.ts, add the lines in **bold**. Note that the credential properties in *firebaseConfig* should be your own (copied from firebase console)

```
import { BrowserModule } from '@angular/platform-browser';
import { ErrorHandler, NgModule } from '@angular/core';
import { IonicApp, IonicErrorHandler, IonicModule } from 'ionic-angular';
import { SplashScreen } from '@ionic-native/splash-screen';
import { StatusBar } from '@ionic-native/status-bar';

import { MyApp } from './app.component';
import { HomePage } from '../pages/home/home';

import { NoteService } from './note.service';
import { IonicStorageModule } from '@ionic/storage';
import { AngularFireModule } from 'angularfire2';
import { AngularFireDatabaseModule } from 'angularfire2/database';

export const firebaseConfig = {
    apiKey: "AIzaSyAonCRyv2DeV75eHxU3GunvbuNpbYqprAY",
    authDomain: "notablenotes-82b3d.firebaseapp.com",
    databaseURL: "https://notablenotes-82b3d.firebaseio.com",
    projectId: "notablenotes-82b3d",
    storageBucket: "notablenotes-82b3d.appspot.com",
    messagingSenderId: "1010273852261"
};
@NgModule({
  declarations: [
    MyApp,
    HomePage
  ],
  imports: [
    BrowserModule,
    IonicModule.forRoot(MyApp),
    IonicStorageModule.forRoot(),
    AngularFireModule.initializeApp(firebaseConfig),
    AngularFireDatabaseModule
  ],
  bootstrap: [IonicApp],
  entryComponents: [
```

```
    MyApp,
    HomePage
  ],
  providers: [
    StatusBar,
    SplashScreen,
    NoteService,
    {provide: ErrorHandler, useClass: IonicErrorHandler}
  ]
})
export class AppModule {}
```

Code Explanation

```
import { AngularFireModule } from 'angularfire2';
import { AngularFireDatabaseModule } from 'angularfire2/database';
```

angularfire2 is a library that sits on top of firebase and makes it easier to build Angular apps that use firebase as the backend as we will see shortly.

home.ts

Now to make sure that we have added firebase correctly to our project, go to home.ts and add the lines in **bold**.

```
import { Component } from '@angular/core';
import { NavController } from 'ionic-angular';

import { NoteService } from '../../app/note.service';
import { AngularFireDatabase } from 'angularfire2/database';

@Component({
  selector: 'page-home',
  templateUrl: 'home.html'
})
export class HomePage {

  notes;

  constructor(public    navCtrl:    NavController,    private    noteService:
NoteService, db: AngularFireDatabase) {
    console.log(db);
  }
```

Make sure that the lite web server is running (by executing *ionic serve*) and in the console, you should see the *AngularFireDatabase* object printed as shown below to prove that we have added Angular Fire correctly.

```
▼ AngularFireDatabase ⊡
  ▶ app: e
  ▶ database: Pg
  ▶ __proto__: Object
```

7.3 Working with a Firebase Database

Now let's look at our Firebase database. Go to console.firebase.google.com. Click on your project, and from the menu bar on the left, click on **Database**.

We will store our data here. If you have not worked with NoSQL databases before, you might find it odd in the beginning because there is no concept of tables or relationships here. Our database is basically a tree of key value pair objects. We basically store json objects here that map natively to json objects in javascript. So when working with a NoSQL database on the backend, we get a json object from the server and we simply display in on the client. Or we construct a json object on the client and send it to server and we store it as it is. There is no additional mapping needed i.e. from relational format to json format or vice-versa.

Click + to add a new child node to the tree. Each node has a name and a value. Value can be a primitive type like string, boolean, number or it can be a complex object.

When you click **Add**, a new node will be added.

```
crudproject-45834
  └── name: "Ervin Lim"
```

(Note that when you add a new child node, the child node gets highlighted in green and the parent node in yellow for a few seconds. If you try deleting a node, that node gets highlighted in red.)

Our values can also be complex objects. You can add complex objects by clicking on the + sign in `Value` of an existing child node. The below tree has a childnode `0` that contains further properties.

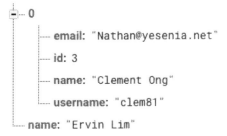

crudproject-45834

```
□ 0
    email: "Nathan@yesenia.net"
    id: 3
    name: "Clement Ong"
    username: "clem81"
    name: "Ervin Lim"
```

You can of course have complex objects in complex, for e.g.

myfirstfirebaseproject-6da6c

```
□ 1
    □ address
        city: "Wisokyburgh"
        □ geo
            lat: "-43.9509"
            lng: "-34.4618"
        street: "Victor Plains"
        suite: "Suite 879"
        zipcode: "90566-7771"
    □ company
        bs: "synergize scalable supply-chains"
        catchPhrase: "Proactive didactic contingency"
        name: "Deckow-Crist"
    email: "Shanna@melissa.tv"
    id: 2
    name: "Ervin Howell"
    phone: "010-692-6593 x09125"
    username: "Antonette"
    website: "anastasia.net"
```

76

Essentially, we have a hierarchy of key value pairs in a NoSQL database. We don't have tables and relationships. The modelling of objects and their relationships vital to an enterprise level application is beyond the scope of this book.

In the next sections, we illustrate the actual C.R.U.D. operations between Firebase and our Ionic app.

7.4 C.R.U.D. Operations on Firebase

7.4.1 Adding a Note

In this section, we will implement adding a note to firebase.

Setting Permissions for Read/Write

Before we implement our 'add note' function, we need to edit our firebase permission rules. In the firebase console, under *Database*, *Rules* tab, our rules are configured (by default) as:

```
{
  "rules": {
    ".read": "auth != null",
    ".write": "auth != null"
  }
}
```

We have a json object that determines the reading and writing of data. The code is saying that read and write permission is only granted to those who are logged in or authenticated (`auth != null`). We will explore firebase authentication and authorization in the next two chapters of the book where we will see how to set these rules to allow certain permissions only to logged in users. But for now, we will make reading and writing public to make things simple.

So in the *Rules* tab, change the permission rules as shown below and click **Publish**. Do note that to make the permissions effective after a change, you need to publish the changes.

```
{
  "rules": {
    ".read": true,
    ".write": true
  }
}
```

note.service.ts

To implement adding to firebase, in NoteService, import and inject *AngularFireDatabase* with the following code in bold:

```
import { Storage } from '@ionic/storage';
import { Injectable } from '@angular/core';

import { AngularFireDatabase } from 'angularfire2/database';

@Injectable()
export class NoteService{

  notes;

  constructor(private storage : Storage, private db:
AngularFireDatabase){
  }
```

Then change *addNote()* to the following implementation:

```
addNote(note){
  this.db.list('/notes/').push({
      title: note.title,
      content: note.content,
      date: note.date
  });
}
```

To add an object to firebase, we use the *push* method from our *AngularFireDatabase this.db.list*. To be able to add an object to firebase, we need to have write permission and we have set this to *true* in the firebase console earlier.

Note that we have specified the location of the node in firebase which we want to add to i.e. '*/notes/*'.

Running Our App

If we run our app now and try to add a note, the newly added note will be reflected in firebase console, *Database, Data* tab (e.g. fig. 7.4.1.1).

figure 7.4.1.1

For now, we are still unable to see our added notes in the home page and that is what we will implement next.

7.4.2 Fetching Notes

Fetching notes from our database is straightforward. In note.service.ts, change your *fetchNotes()* implementation to the below.

note.service.ts

```
fetchNotes(){
   return this.db.list('/notes/');
}
```

Just like for adding notes, we specify the location of the node in firebase ('/notes') where we want to retrieve our data. Notice that we have just one single line of code unlike if we retrieve data using a Promise or Observable (like what we have done for *Storage*). The reason the code is simple is because *AngularFireDatabase.list* returns a *FirebaseListObervable* type which is firebase's own Observable that wraps wround the standard *rxjs* Observable. *FirebaseListObervable* is an *rxjs* Obervable internally but it wraps around it and provides additional methods which makes it easy for us to execute create, read, update and delete functions on it. It is really much simpler to use *FirebaseListObservable*!

79

home.ts

Because we have changed *NoteService fetchNotes()*, we have to change our calling of it in home.ts *ngOnInit* as shown below:

```
ngOnInit(){
    this.notes = this.noteService.fetchNotes();
}
```

home.html

In home.html, we have to apply the 'async' pipe in our *ngFor* to display notes. Because data in *notes* arrive asynchronously, the *async* pipe subscribes to *notes* (which is a FirebaseObjectObservable) and returns the latest value emitted. The *async* pipe marks the component to be checked for changes. It also removes the subscription once the component is destroyed (thus not needing *ngOnDestroy*).

```
<ion-card *ngFor="let note of notes | async" (click)="onItemClick(note)">
```

If we run our app now, you should be able to see the list of notes that you have added in home page when you start up your app (figure 7.4.2.1).

figure 7.4.2.1

80

7.4.3 Editing a Note

Next, we want to implement editing a note in firebase.

First implement *editNote()* in NoteService as shown below.

note.service.ts

```
editNote(note){
   this.db.object('/notes/'+note.$key).update({
       title: note.title,
       content: note.content,
       date: note.date
   });
}
```

Code Explanation

To edit a specific note, we need to first specify the location of the data in the *object()* method.

```
this.db.object('/notes/'+note.$key)
```

In our case the location of the object is contained in the *$key* property of the *note* object we have clicked to edit. How did we get this *$key* property? Whenever we add an object to firebase, a unique key is generated for us.

```
notablenotes-82b3d
├─ notes
│   ├─ -Kk9CtiZ6BbBvGWNhsFv
│   │     ├─ content: "Real time adding!"
│   │     ├─ date: "2017-01-01"
│   │     └─ title: "My First Note on Ionic"
│   └─ -Kk9GRjwPJ1sldBtn-Uw
│         ├─ content: "Firebase makes it so easy to have a backend for..."
│         ├─ date: "2017-07-01"
│         └─ title: "My Second Note on Firebase"
```

figure 7.4.3.1

For example, we have the unique keys *Kk9CtiZ6BbBvGWNhsFv* and *Kk9GRjwPJ1sIdBtn-Uw* generated for the two notes that I have added (fig. 7.4.3.1). The unique key of a single object is stored in *$key* which can be used to retrieve the object for update and also for retrieval and deletion as we will implement later.

```
this.db.object('/notes/'+note.$key).update({
```

Having specified the targeted object using `this.db.object('/notes/'+note.$key)`, we call the *update()* method to update the object in firebase.

detail.ts

Having implemented *editNote*, we then call it in detail.ts in *ionViewWillLeave()* as shown below in **bold**. Note that we no longer call *writeToStorage()* since all data is stored in firebase.

```
ionViewWillLeave() {

    if(this.note.title === "" && this.note.date === "" &&
this.note.content === ""){
        // if note is blank don't do anything
    }
    else if(this.newNoteFlag){
      this.noteService.addNote(this.note);
      console.log("add note");
    }
    else if(this.deleteNoteFlag){
      this.noteService.removeNote(this.note);
      console.log("delete note");
    }
    else{
      this.noteService.editNote(this.note);
      console.log("edit note");
    }
  }
```

7.4.4 Deleting Notes

Next, we want to implement deleting a note from firebase.

note.service.ts

We first change the implementation of *removeNote()* in NoteService as shown below.

```
removeNote(note){
  this.db.object('/notes/'+note.$key).remove()
    .then( x=> console.log("SUCCESS"))
    .catch( error => {
      alert("Could not delete note.");
      console.log("ERROR", error)
    });
}
```

Code Explanation

Similar to editing a specific note, deleting a note involves specifying the location of the data in the *object()* method with the *$key* property of the *note* object we have clicked to delete.

```
this.db.object('/notes/'+note.$key).remove()
```

We specify the targeted object using `this.db.object('/notes/'+note.$key)` and call the *remove()* method to remove it from firebase. Note that *remove()* returns a Promise you can optionally subscribe to be notified if the deletion is successful (the same applies for *push()* and *update()*).

```
this.db.object('/notes/'+note.$key).remove()
  .then( x=> console.log("SUCCESS"))
  .catch( error => {
    alert("Could not delete note.");
    console.log("ERROR", error)
  });
```

If successful, we log "SUCCESS" and if an error is caught, we log an error message.

No change is needed in detail.ts since we are already calling *removeNote()* upon *deleteNoteFlag* being set to true.

Running your App

If you run your app now, it should have full functionality to create, update, delete and read notes data from and to firebase.

Summary

In this chapter, we learnt how to implement C.R.U.D. operations using Firebase as our backend. We learnt how to add firebase to our application, how to work with the firebase database from the firebase console, how to set permissions for read/write, how to fetch our notes, how to add a note with the push method, how to delete a note with the remove method and how to update a note. You can access the full code for this chapter at https://github.com/greglim81/ionic-chapter7

In the next chapter, we will explore Firebase's login authentication feature.

CHAPTER 8: AUTHENTICATION IN FIREBASE

We have learnt how to store and fetch data from firebase. The problem however now is that our app is limited to a single user. Suppose we want our app to be used by multiple users and each user should only have access to their own notes. To do this, we need to authenticate users before they can view or edit any data.

8.1 Adding a Login Page

We will start by adding a new login page. We will use the Ionic CLI to add a new page. From inside the project folder, run

```
ionic generate page login
```

The above command creates all the necessary files for the login page. There will now be a *login* folder with some boiler plate code.

We want the login page to be displayed first when a user opens it. To do so, set Login page to be the root page by seting *rootPage* in App component to *Login* as shown in **bold** below:

```
export class MyApp {
  rootPage:any = 'Login';
```

We next design login.html. We will use Floating labels this time around (Read more about Floating labels at https://ionicframework.com/docs/components/#floating-labels). In the Ionic documentation, copy the sample code and paste it in login.html.

```
<ion-header>
  <ion-navbar>
    <ion-title>login</ion-title>
  </ion-navbar>
</ion-header>


<ion-content padding>
  <ion-list>
    <ion-item>
      <ion-label floating>Username</ion-label>
      <ion-input type="text"></ion-input>
    </ion-item>
```

```
    <ion-item>
      <ion-label floating>Password</ion-label>
      <ion-input type="password"></ion-input>
    </ion-item>
  </ion-list>
</ion-content>
```

The sample code has two fields username and password which is what we need exactly for a login page. We will bind these two fields to the *username* and *password* property in login.ts which we will define later. But first, apply the *ngModel* directive on both two input fields for two-way binding as shown below in bold.

```
    <ion-item>
      <ion-label fixed>Username</ion-label>
      <ion-input type="text" [(ngModel)]="username" ></ion-input>
    </ion-item>

    <ion-item>
      <ion-label fixed>Password</ion-label>
      <ion-input type="password" [(ngModel)]="password"></ion-input>
    </ion-item>
```

We also add a basic sign in button at the bottom just before the close of </*ion-content*> as shown below. We bind it to the *signIn()* method which we will shortly implement.

```
  </ion-list>
  <button ion-button (click)="signIn()">Login</button>
</ion-content>
```

login.ts

In login.ts, declare the two variables *username* and *password*

```
export class Login {

  username = '';
  password = '';



```

Then implement the *signIn()* method:

86

```
signIn(){
  console.log(this.username + ' ' + this.password);
}
```

8.2 Firebase Authentication

Our *signIn* method currently does not do anything except printing to the console. To implement authentication, we first need to enable authentication for our app in firebase console. Go to *Authentication, Sign-In Method* and enable *'Email and Password'* sign-in provider (fig. 8.2.1).

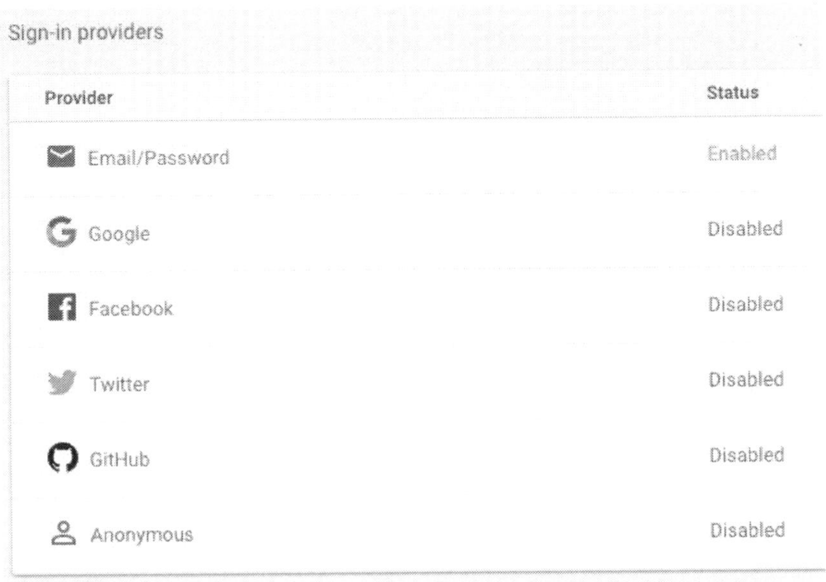

Sign-in providers

Provider	Status
✉ Email/Password	Enabled
G Google	Disabled
f Facebook	Disabled
🐦 Twitter	Disabled
○ GitHub	Disabled
👤 Anonymous	Disabled

figure 8.2.1

app.module.ts

We next need to import *AngularFireAuthModule* and *AuthService* (which we will implement later) in App module. Add the lines in **bold** below to app.module.ts.

...

```
import { NoteService } from './note.service';
import { IonicStorageModule } from '@ionic/storage';
import { AngularFireModule } from 'angularfire2';
```

```
import { AngularFireDatabaseModule } from 'angularfire2/database';
import { AngularFireAuthModule } from 'angularfire2/auth';
import { AuthService } from './auth.service';

export const firebaseConfig = {
    ...
};
@NgModule({
  declarations: [
    MyApp,
    HomePage
  ],
  imports: [
    BrowserModule,
    IonicModule.forRoot(MyApp),
    IonicStorageModule.forRoot(),
    AngularFireModule.initializeApp(firebaseConfig),
    AngularFireDatabaseModule,
    AngularFireAuthModule
  ],
  ...
  ...
  providers: [
    StatusBar,
    SplashScreen,
    NoteService,
    AuthService,
    {provide: ErrorHandler, useClass: IonicErrorHandler}
  ]
})
export class AppModule {}
```

AngularFireAuthModule is the individual authentication module that we need to add after adding the *AngularFireModule*. Other modules in *AngularFire* include the *AngularFireDatabaseModule* which we have used earlier to access the firebase database, and *AngularFireStorageModule* and *AngularFireMessageModule*.

auth.service.ts

Next, we create an Authentication Service auth.service.ts under /*app* with the below code.

```
import { Injectable } from '@angular/core';
import { AngularFireAuth } from 'angularfire2/auth';

@Injectable()
```

```
export class AuthService{

  constructor(private afAuth: AngularFireAuth){
  }

  signIn(username: string, password: string){
      return this.afAuth.auth.signInWithEmailAndPassword(username,password);
  }
}
```

signInWithEmailAndPassword asynchronously signs in using email and password and fails with an error if the email address and password do not match.

login.ts

In login.ts, add the codes in **bold**.

```
import { Component } from '@angular/core';
import { IonicPage, NavController, NavParams } from 'ionic-angular';

import { AuthService } from '../../app/auth.service';

@IonicPage()
@Component({
  selector: 'page-login',
  templateUrl: 'login.html',
})
export class Login {

  username = '';
  password = '';

  constructor(public navCtrl: NavController, public navParams: NavParams,
private authService: AuthService) {
  }

  signIn(){
    this.authService.signIn(this.username,this.password)
      .then(authState => {
        console.log("Login-then",authState);
      })
      .catch(function(error) {
        // Handle Errors here.
        //var errorCode = error.code;
        var errorMessage = error.message;
        console.log(error);
      });
```

```
    }
}
```

In *signIn()*, we call *authService.signIn* which asynchronously signs in using email and password. If the login fails, we log the *error* object returned.

Testing our Authentication

If you run your app now and try to login with an invalid email as username, you get the below error message:

code: "auth/invalid-email", message: "The email address is badly formatted."

Or if you login with an invalid account, you get the below error:

code: "auth/user-not-found", message: "There is no user record corresponding to this identifier. The user may have been deleted."

At this point, we have not implemented our sign up function yet. But you can create a user account direct in firebase console. Proceed to create a test user like in fig. 8.2.2.

figure 8.2.2

Once you have created your test user in firebase console, try logging in again with the user credentials and you should be able to login successfully with the below message:

Login-then   U   {ba: Array(0),   j: "AIzaSyAonCRyv2DeV75eHxU3GunvbuNpbYqprAY",   D: "[DEFAULT]", v: "notablenotes-82b3d.firebaseapp.com", g: S…}

8.3 Forward to Homepage

When a user signs in successfully, we want to direct her to the home page. To do so, import *HomePage* with the below line.

```
import { HomePage } from '../home/home';
```

Next, add the line in **bold** to the *then* clause of *signIn*.

```
this.authService.signIn(this.username,this.password)
  .then(authState => {
      console.log("Login-then",authState);
      this.navCtrl.setRoot(HomePage);
  })
  .catch(function(error) {
    // Handle Errors here.
    //var errorCode = error.code;
    var errorMessage = error.message;
    console.log(error);
  });
```

When a user logins successfully now, she is brought to the home page. Essentially we can choose which screen you want to redirect the user to when the app starts by specifying it in *setRoot*.

Loading and Alert Pop Up

Next, we want to show a Loading pop up when a user logins (while waiting for the response) and an alert pop up when the login fails. In login.ts, add the codes in **bold** shown below:

```
import { Component } from '@angular/core';
import { IonicPage, NavController, LoadingController, AlertController } from
'ionic-angular';

import { AuthService } from '../../app/auth.service';

import { HomePage } from '../home/home';

@IonicPage()
@Component({
  selector: 'page-login',
  templateUrl: 'login.html',
})
export class Login {

  username = '';
  password = '';

  constructor(public navCtrl: NavController, private authService: AuthService,
```

91

```
    private loadingCtrl: LoadingController, private alertCtrl: AlertController) {
  }

  signIn(){
    const loading = this.loadingCtrl.create({
      content: 'Signing you in...'
    });
    loading.present();

    this.authService.signIn(this.username,this.password)
      .then(authState => {
          loading.dismiss();
          this.navCtrl.setRoot(HomePage);
      })
      .catch(error => {
          loading.dismiss();
          const alert = this.alertCtrl.create({
            title: 'Signin failed.',
            message: error.message,
            buttons:['Ok']
          });
          alert.present();
      })
  }
}
```

We use the Loading Controller to show a loading screen with message 'signing you in...'. When the sign in is successful, we dismiss the loading screen. If the sign in fails, we dismiss it as well but show an Alert Controller with the error message thrown.

Next, we will implement our Sign Up screen.

8.4 Sign Up Page

A login page typically displays a sign up link for a user who does not have an existing account. In login.html, add the below codes in **bold** to display a sign up link.

```
<ion-header>
  <ion-navbar>
    <ion-title>Login</ion-title>
    <ion-buttons end>
      <button ion-button (click)="signUp()">
        Sign Up
      </button>
    </ion-buttons>
  </ion-navbar>
</ion-header>
```

With the *ion-buttons* component, we add our sign up button to the header toolbars. This component wraps one or more buttons, and can be given the *start* or *end* attributes to control the placement of the buttons it contains. In our case, we use the *end* attribute to place the signup button at the end of the toolbar (fig. 8.4.1).

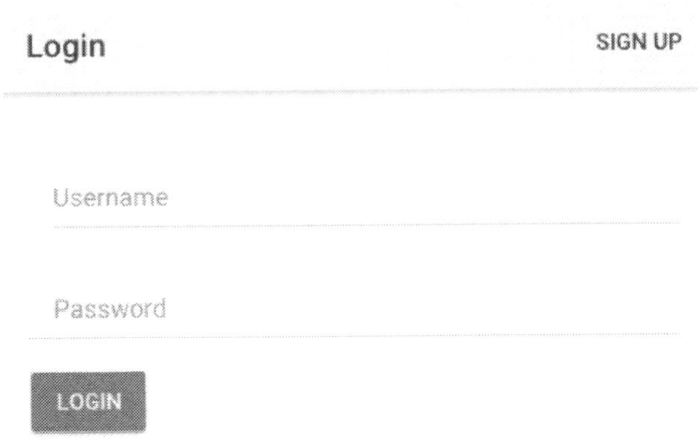

Login   SIGN UP

Username

Password

LOGIN

figure 8.4.1

In Terminal, run

```
ionic generate page signup
```

to generate our sign up page just as what we have done with login page before.

When the *signup* folder is generated by Ionic CLI, in login.ts, implement *signUp()* as shown:

```
signUp(){
    this.navCtrl.setRoot('Signup');
}
```

Now when you click 'Signup' in Login, you will be brought to the sign up page. Notice how easy it is to generate pages using the Ionic CLI and navigate to them!

signup.html

Our signup.html will be very similar to login.html (i.e. username and password fields). Copy the code from login.html and paste it into signup.html and change the codes shown in **bold** below.

```html
<ion-header>
  <ion-navbar>
    <ion-title>Sign Up</ion-title>
  </ion-navbar>
</ion-header>

<ion-content padding>
  <ion-list>
    <ion-item>
      <ion-label floating>Username</ion-label>
      <ion-input type="text" [(ngModel)]="username"></ion-input>
    </ion-item>

    <ion-item>
      <ion-label floating>Password</ion-label>
      <ion-input type="password" [(ngModel)]="password"></ion-input>
    </ion-item>
  </ion-list>
  <button ion-button (click)=" onSignUp()">Sign Up</button>
</ion-content>
```

auth.service.ts

```typescript
import { Injectable } from '@angular/core';
import { AngularFireAuth } from 'angularfire2/auth';

@Injectable()
export class AuthService{

  constructor(private afAuth: AngularFireAuth){
  }

  signIn(username: string, password: string){
      return this.afAuth.auth.signInWithEmailAndPassword(username,password);
  }

  signup(username: string, password: string){
      return this.afAuth.auth.createUserWithEmailAndPassword(username,password);
  }

}
```

`afAuth.auth.createUserWithEmailAndPassword` encodes our data and sends it to a RESTful api on Google server to create a user for us. The newly created user can be seen in the firebase console authentication list (fig. 8.4.2).

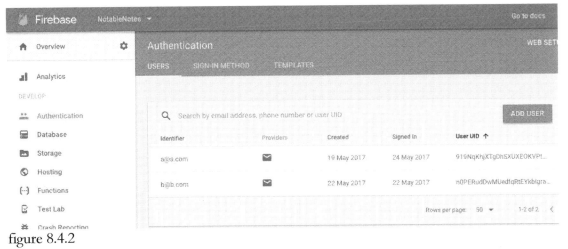

figure 8.4.2

signup.ts

Lastly, fill in signup.ts with the below codes:

```
import { Component } from '@angular/core';
import { IonicPage, NavController, LoadingController, AlertController }
from 'ionic-angular';
import { AuthService } from '../../app/auth.service';

import { HomePage } from '../home/home';

@IonicPage()
@Component({
  selector: 'page-signup',
  templateUrl: 'signup.html',
})
export class Signup {

  username = '';
  password = '';

  constructor(private    authService:    AuthService,    public    navCtrl:
NavController, private loadingCtrl: LoadingController, private alertCtrl:
AlertController) {
  }

  onSignUp(){

    const loading = this.loadingCtrl.create({
```

```
      content: 'Signing you up...'
    });
    loading.present();

    this.authService.signup(this.username, this.password)
      .then(
        data => {
          loading.dismiss()
          this.navCtrl.setRoot(HomePage);
        }
      ) // successfully create new user
      .catch(
        error => {
          loading.dismiss();
        // display error in a alert
          const alert = this.alertCtrl.create({
            title: 'Signup failed',
            message: error.message,
            buttons: ['Ok']
          });
          alert.present();

        } // potential errors
      ); // result is a promise
  }
}
```

Code Explanation

The implementation of signup.ts is very similar to login.html. We import the same classes, *LoadingController*, *AlertController*, *AuthService* and *HomePage* and inject them in the constructor. *onSignUp()* looks almost the same as *signIn()* except that we call *authService.signup* instead of *signIn*.

Running your App

When you run your app now and sign up a new user, this new user will reflect in the firebase console - *Authentication*, under *Users*.

And if you try signing up with the same email address twice, you get the error message:

Signup failed

The email address is already in
use by another account.

OK

8.5 Managing the User State.

Now, we want an already authenticated user to go straight to the Home page instead of having to login each time they open the app. To do this, we implement *getAuthState* in auth.service.ts as shown below:

```
getCurrentUser(){
    return this.afAuth.authState;
}
```

afAuth.authState returns an *Observable<firebase.User>* to monitor our application's authentication State if there is a logged in user. If it will returns null, it means the user have been logged out. With this, we subscribe to *getAuthState* in app component to determine which root page to show to logged in/out users.

app.component.ts

In app.component.ts, add the codes in **bold** shown below.

```
import { Component } from '@angular/core';
import { Platform } from 'ionic-angular';
import { StatusBar } from '@ionic-native/status-bar';
import { SplashScreen } from '@ionic-native/splash-screen';

import { HomePage } from '../pages/home/home';
import { AuthService } from './auth.service';

@Component({
  templateUrl: 'app.html'
})
export class MyApp {
  rootPage:any = 'Login';

  user;
```

```
constructor(platform:    Platform,   statusBar:   StatusBar,   splashScreen:
SplashScreen, private authService: AuthService) {
    this.authService.getCurrentUser().subscribe(authState => {
      if(authState){
        this.rootPage = HomePage;
        console.log("logged in as " + authState.uid);
      }
      else{
        this.rootPage = 'Login';
      }
    });
    platform.ready().then(() => {
      // Okay, so the platform is ready and our plugins are available.
      // Here you can do any higher level native things you might need.
      statusBar.styleDefault();
      splashScreen.hide();
    });
  }
}
```

Code Explanation

We subscribe to *authState* and if *authState* exists, we set root page to *home* and log the authenticated user id. If *authState* is null, there is no authenticated user and we display the login page.

8.6 Logging Users Out

In auth.service.ts, implemenent the logout() method as shown:

```
logout(){
    this.afAuth.auth.signOut();
}
```

In home.html, we display a logout button.

```
<ion-header>
  <ion-navbar>
    <ion-title>
      Notable Notes
    </ion-title>
    <ion-buttons end>
      <button ion-button (click)="logout()">
```

```
        Logout
      </button>
    </ion-buttons>
  </ion-navbar>
</ion-header>
```

In home.ts, implement logout() as shown below (remember to import and inject AuthService)

```
logout(){
  this.authService.logout();
  this.navCtrl.setRoot('Login');
}
```

Running our App

If we run our app now and if we are logged in, we will be brought to the home page. If you click logout, you will be logged out and brought to the login page. And when you reload this time round, you will be brought to the login page since you have already logged out.

How Firebase Authenticates

Authentication in our Ionic app and firebase happens by we first sending authentication credentials to the server (email, password). The server checks the credentials if they are valid and generates a token and return this token to the client. The client stores this token and on each request to a protected resource on the server, will resend the token to the server. The token proves that a client has already authenticated with the server some time ago and the server can check if its valid. If the token is valid, the client will request the server to provide access to whatever protected resource the client is trying to access. Naturally, such tokens also invalidate after a couple of minutes or hours. This is the approach used internally by firebase in our Ionic apps.

If we run our app in the browser, we can see that firebase stores the token in *Local Storage* of browser. If you go to 'Chrome developer tools', 'Application', 'Storage', 'Local Storage', 'localhost:8100' (figure...), you can see the key and value of the generated token.

Initially before we login, there are no key-value pairs (fig. 8.6.1).

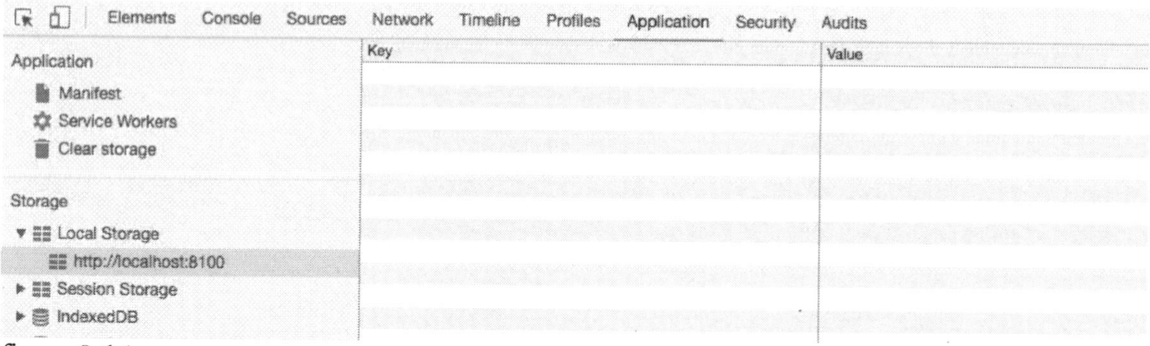

figure 8.6.1

If you login now, you will see a new key-value pair token generated (fig. 8.6.2):

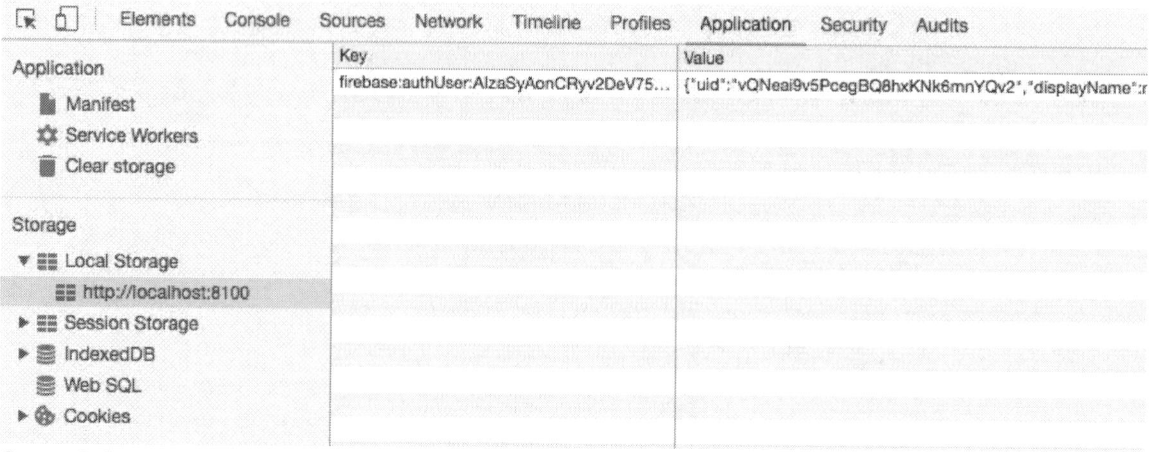

figure 8.6.2

And if you logout, the token is deleted.

Summary

In this chapter, we learnt how to implement authentication using firebase to support multiple users for our app. We added a login page, a sign up page and an Authentication service to our project. Hopefully, we should now have a better understanding of how to implement authentication using firebase authentication.

You can access the full code for this chapter at https://github.com/greglim81/ionic-chapter8and9

CHAPTER 9: AUTHORIZATION IN FIREBASE

Having covered authentication in firebase, we will go on to authorization in firebase.

In authentication, we authenticate users for who they claim to be. In authorization, we determine what a user is allowed to do after they have been authenticated e.g. the pages that they are allowed to view or if they are allowed to modify certain data.

Our database rules are currently set as:

```
{
  "rules": {
    ".read": true,
    ".write": true
  }
}
```

This means that anyone can read or write to our database. Having implemented authentication login and signup, we should now change our rules back to the default:

```
{
  "rules": {
    ".read": "auth != null",
    ".write": "auth != null"
  }
}
```

(note that whenever you change rules in firebase console, you need to 'publish' to apply it)

This allows full read and write access to only authenticated users of your app. Which is to say, our home page or detail is not visible to users who are not logged in.

We have a problem however. Our app currently only allows one user. If we want our app to have multiple users, we would need to further improve our data structure and also specify authorization rules such that a user can only access her own notes.

Implementing for Multiple Users

Our notes are currently stored in the database node *notes*. To allow for multiple users, under *notes* node, we will have a child node for each user. Each child node is represented by the *uid* of the user. A uid is the user's unique identifier. The below structure illustrates this:

notablenodes
  --notes
    --uid1
        --note1
        --note2
        ...
    --uid2
        --note1
        --note2
        ...
    ...

In this way, each user will only have access to his own *uid* node.

9.1 Working with Security Rules for Multiple Users

To specify authorization rules for our data structure, will need to set our rules as:

```
{
  "rules": {
    "notes":{
      "$uid":{
        ".read": "auth.uid === $uid",
        ".write": "auth.uid === $uid",
      }
    }
  }
}
```

We apply a rule to each *uid* node in *notes* node. With our rules, we specify that an authenticated user can only read or write to the node whose *uid* equals the user's *uid*.

What if we want to apply different rules for different nodes? For example, we want the *Home* page to be accessible to all authenticated users, the *About* page to be accessible to the public (including unauthenticated users) and only the *notes* node for each individual user. We could set up our rules like this:

```
{
  "rules": {
    "notes":{
      "$uid":{
        ".read": "auth.uid === $uid",
        ".write": "auth.uid === $uid",
      }
    },
    "home":{
        ".read": "auth != null",
        ".write": "auth != null",
    },
    "about":{
        ".read": true,
        ".write": true,
    }
  }
}
```

In this way, in addition to each user having access only to their own node, all logged in users have access to the *home* node and all users whether logged in or not have access to the *about* node.

Rules are Cascading

Do note that rules are cascading. Which means, any rule applied to the parent node will apply to its child nodes. For example, if I add the below two rules to the root node, that means all child nodes will be publically available for reading and writing. This also renders all the other child specific authentication rules as useless. So make sure that your parent node does not have rules which override your child rules rendering them ineffective.

```
{
  "rules": {
    ".read": true,
    ".write": true,
    "products":{
      "$uid":{
        ".read": "auth.uid === $uid",
        ".write": "auth.uid === $uid",
      }
    },
    "home":{
        ".read": "auth != null",
        ".write": "auth != null",
```

```
    },
    "about":{
        ".read": true,
        ".write": true,
    }
  }
}
```

9.2 Using the Rules Simulator

Without having to manually test it in our code, we can simulate 'read' or 'write' operations and see if they act according to our expectations in the Simulator.

To do so, first choose the location of the node which we want to try operating on in the *Location* field. For example, to choose the *notes* node, I specify */notes* in *Location* (fig. 9.2.1).

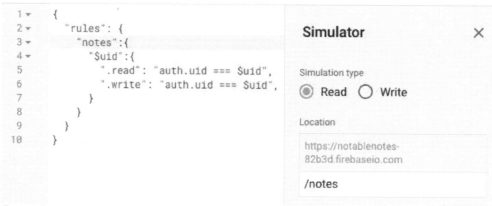

figure 9.2.1

Next, you can set if authenticated or not. If you set authenticated on, you will be prompted to select a Provider, and also specify a unique identifier *uid* which represents a particular user or server.

Once done, you can run to see if the operation is allowed or not. For example, I can specify that I want to run a read operation on a specific node with a particular uid. If I set authenticated and *uid* to be the same, I get a success and a tick highlighting the line that allowed the read operation (fig. 9.2.2).

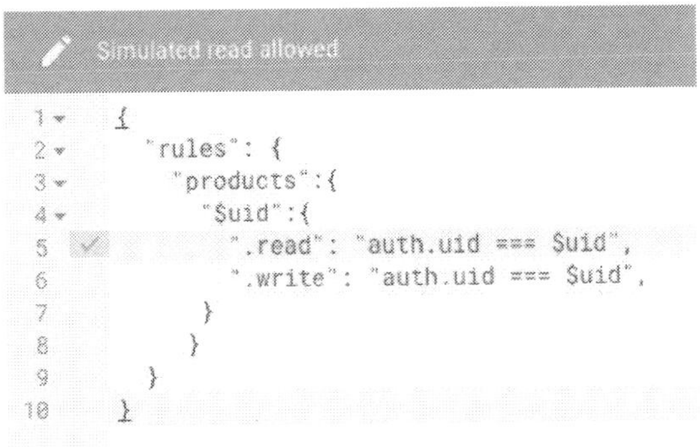

```
 1 ▾    {
 2 ▾       "rules": {
 3 ▾          "products":{
 4 ▾             "$uid":{
 5 ✓               ".read": "auth.uid === $uid",
 6                  ".write": "auth.uid === $uid",
 7               }
 8            }
 9         }
10     }
```

figure 9.2.2

But if I try to access the same node this time with a different *uid* to represent a different user (fig. 9.2.3),

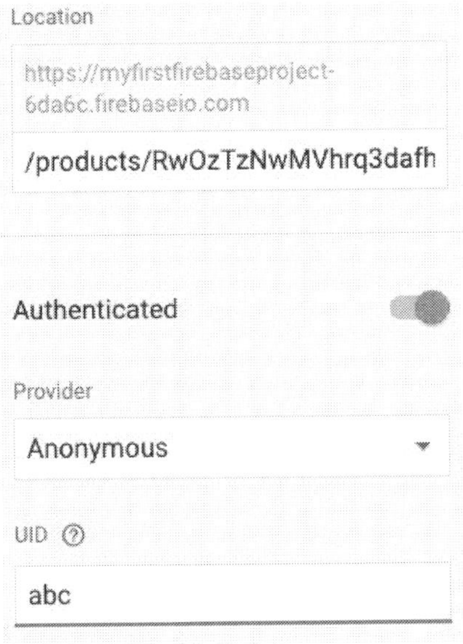

Location

https://myfirstfirebaseproject-
6da6c.firebaseio.com

/products/RwOzTzNwMVhrq3dafh

Authenticated

Provider

Anonymous

UID ⓘ

abc

figure 9.2.3

My operation is denied with the simulator showing the line that denied the access. This means that a different user cannot access that user node (fig. 9.2.4).

```
     ✎  Simulated read denied

 1 ▾  {
 2 ▾      "rules": {
 3 ▾        "products":{
 4 ▾          "$uid":{
 5  ✕          ".read": "auth.uid === $uid",
 6              ".write": "auth.uid === $uid",
 7            }
 8          }
 9        }
10  }
```

figure 9.2.4

So the simulator is useful for us to test our rules before we publish our application.

9.3 Implementing Multiple Users

Having set our authorization rules, we now make the necessary changes to our code. The main change to our code is that we have to include the current logged in user id whenever we execute a create, read, update or delete operation.

So in note.service.ts add *userId* as an argument to the methods and append it to the node location as shown in bold below:

```
import { Storage } from '@ionic/storage';
import { Injectable } from '@angular/core';

import { AngularFireDatabase } from 'angularfire2/database';

@Injectable()
export class NoteService{

  notes;

  constructor(private storage : Storage, private db:
AngularFireDatabase){
  }

  fetchNotes(userId){
    return this.db.list('/notes/'+userId);
  }
```

106

```
removeNote(note,userId){
  this.db.object('/notes/'+userId+'/'+note.$key).remove()
    .then( x=> console.log("SUCCESS"))
    .catch( error => {
      alert("Could not delete note.");
      console.log("ERROR", error)
    });
}

addNote(note,userId){
  this.db.list('/notes/'+userId).push({
      title: note.title,
      content: note.content,
      date: note.date
  });
}

editNote(note,userId){
  this.db.object('/notes/'+userId+'/'+note.$key).update({
      title: note.title,
      content: note.content,
      date: note.date
  });
}
}
```

Essentially, we don't read/write to *notes* node itself, but read/write to the *userId* child node in *notes* instead therefore allowing multiple users.

home.ts

In home.ts, add the codes in **bold** shown below.

```
export class HomePage {

  notes;
  userId;

  constructor(public    navCtrl:    NavController,    private    noteService:
NoteService, db: AngularFireDatabase, private authService: AuthService) {
    console.log(db);
  }

  ngOnInit(){
    this.authService.getCurrentUser().subscribe(authState => {
```

```
      this.userId = authState.uid;
      this.notes = this.noteService.fetchNotes(this.userId);
    });
  }

  onItemClick(note){
    this.navCtrl. push('Detail',{
      noteParam : note,
      userId : this.userId
    });
  }

  onAddClick(){
    this.navCtrl.push('Detail',{
      userId : this.userId
    });
  }

  logout(){
    this.authService.logout();
    this.navCtrl.setRoot('Login');
  }
}
```

Similar to what we do in App component, we retrieve the *userId* from Auth service and pass in *userId* as argument to *fetchNotes* method in Note service in *ngOnInit*. We also pass *userId* as a navigation parameter to detail page in *onItemClick* and *onAddClick*

detail.ts

Finally, in detail.ts, make the code changes as shown below:

```
import { Component } from '@angular/core';
import { IonicPage, NavController, NavParams, AlertController } from
'ionic-angular';

import { NoteService } from '../../app/note.service';

@IonicPage()
@Component({
  selector: 'page-detail',
  templateUrl: 'detail.html',
})
export class Detail {
```

```
  note;
  userId;
  newNoteFlag = false;
  deleteNoteFlag = false;

  constructor(public navCtrl: NavController, public navParams: NavParams,
private noteService: NoteService, private alertCtrl: AlertController) {
      this.note = this.navParams.get('noteParam');
      this.userId = this.navParams.get('userId');
      if(!this.note){
        this.note = {
          id: '',
          date: '',
          title: '',
          content: ''
        };
        this.newNoteFlag = true;
      }
  }

  onTrash(){
      ...
  }

  ionViewWillLeave() {

      if(this.note.title   ===   ""   &&   this.note.date   ===   ""   &&
this.note.content === ""){
        // if note is blank don't do anything
      }
      else if(this.newNoteFlag){
        this.noteService.addNote(this.note, this.userId);
      }
      else if(this.deleteNoteFlag){
        this.noteService.removeNote(this.note, this.userId);
      }
      else{
        this.noteService.editNote(this.note, this.userId);
      }
  }
}
```

Here, we simply retrieve *userId* from *navParams* and pass it as argument to *addNote*, *removeNote* and *editNote* of Note Service.

Running the App

If we run the app now, we find that we can now add notes for each specific user. If you create multiple user accounts, each user account can only read/write to her own notes. Our app can now enable multiple users to create their own notes!

Summary

In this chapter, we learnt how to configure database security rules and also how to use the Firebase Rules Simulator to manage authorization for multiple users in our app. You can access the full code for this chapter at https://github.com/greglim81/ionic-chapter8and9

CHAPTER 10: CORDOVA PLUGINS AND IONIC NATIVE

Cordova plugins as explained in https://cordova.apache.org/plugins/ are:

bits of add-on code that provides JavaScript interface to native components. They allow your app to use native device capabilities beyond what is available to pure web apps.

A Cordova plugin takes a native functionality and makes it available as a Javascript API that we can use in our app. In general, Cordova plugins are only available when we run our project as an Android or iOS app. If we run it as a mobile website or progressive webapp, the plugins won't work.

Before we can use any plugin functionality, we need to add that plugin into that project. Projects generated with the CLI already includes some commonly used plugins. We can see which ones have been included by typing:

```
ionic cordova plugin list
```

(If you are still using the v2 CLI and can't update for whatever reason, just remove the *cordova* before *plugin*. i.e. `ionic plugin list`. This applies to following commands that we will execute later to add our plugins.)

Output:

```
cordova-plugin-console 1.0.5 "Console"
cordova-plugin-device 1.1.4 "Device"
cordova-plugin-splashscreen 4.0.3 "Splashscreen"
cordova-plugin-statusbar 2.2.2 "StatusBar"
cordova-plugin-whitelist 1.3.1 "Whitelist"
cordova-sqlite-storage 2.0.4 "Cordova sqlite storage plugin"
ionic-plugin-keyboard 2.2.1 "Keyboard"
```

Notice that included is the cordova splashscreen plugin. If we look at the root component of our app, *app.component.ts*, in the constructor, we call the *hide* method of *Splashscreen* plugin. This hides the splash screen when our app is ready.

```
import { Component } from '@angular/core';
import { Platform } from 'ionic-angular';
import { StatusBar, Splashscreen } from 'ionic-native';
```

```
import { TabsPage } from '../pages/tabs/tabs';


@Component({
  templateUrl: 'app.html'
})
export class MyApp {
  rootPage = TabsPage;

  constructor(platform: Platform) {
    platform.ready().then(() => {
      // Okay, so the platform is ready and our plugins are available.
      // Here you can do any higher level native things you might need.
      StatusBar.styleDefault();
      Splashscreen.hide();
    });
  }
}
```

You might notice here that we use the *Splashscreen* class imported from *ionic native*. And in *package.json*, *ionic-native* is a package listed in our project dependencies.

```
"dependencies": {
  "@angular/common": "4.0.2",
  ...
  "@ionic-native/core": "3.6.1",
  "@ionic-native/splash-screen": "3.6.1",
  "@ionic-native/status-bar": "3.6.1",
  "@ionic/storage": "^2.0.1",
  "angularfire2": "^4.0.0-rc.0",
  "firebase": "^3.9.0",
  "ionic-angular": "3.1.1",
  "ionicons": "3.0.0",
  "rxjs": "5.1.1",
  "sw-toolbox": "3.4.0",
  "uuid": "^3.0.1",
  "zone.js": "^0.8.10"  },
```

As described in the Ionic Documentation about Ionic Native: *Ionic Native is a curated set of ES5/ES6/TypeScript wrappers for Cordova/PhoneGap plugins that make adding any native functionality you need to your Ionic, Cordova, or Web View mobile app easy.*

Also, if the plugin uses asynchronous operations with callbacks, Ionic Native converts them into Promises and Observables that we can work with in our code.

You can find out what available plugins there are by going to:
https://ionicframework.com/docs/native/

10.1 Installing a Cordova Plugin

We have seen that we can use Cordova plugins and Ionic Native to add access to native mobile functionality that is not available to web apps.

We will illustrate plugins by creating a new Ionic tabs project which uses the Camera plugin in the default 'about' tab and the Google Map plugin in the default 'Home' tab. A tab-based application is a very common type of application that uses a tabs-based navigation system.

Create the new tabs project by running:

```
ionic start PluginExample tabs
```

Next, to install the Camera plugin to our project, we run (as mentioned in Ionic docs):

```
ionic cordova plugin add cordova-plugin-camera

npm install --save @ionic-native/camera
```

(Remember, that if you are still using the v2 CLI and can't update for whatever reason, just remove the *cordova* before *plugin*)

The plugin name is `cordova-plugin-camera`. Most plugins follow this naming convention where they are called *cordova-plugin-<something>*. After the installation of the plugin, we can use it in our code.

10.2 Using the Camera Plugin

After adding the cordova camera plugin in our app, we are ready to use it in our app. We have to test our changes in either Android simulator or iOS emulator because the plugin won't work in Chrome. In the following, we will run it in the iOS simulator. We run our app with the --*livereload* option so that our app will automatically update whenever there is a code change. Execute the below to run our app in the iOS emulator:

ionic cordova emulate ios --livereload

This will open the iOS emulator with our app running (fig. 10.2.1). Now, before we dwell into the specifics of plugins, let's first explore the tabs template.

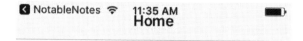

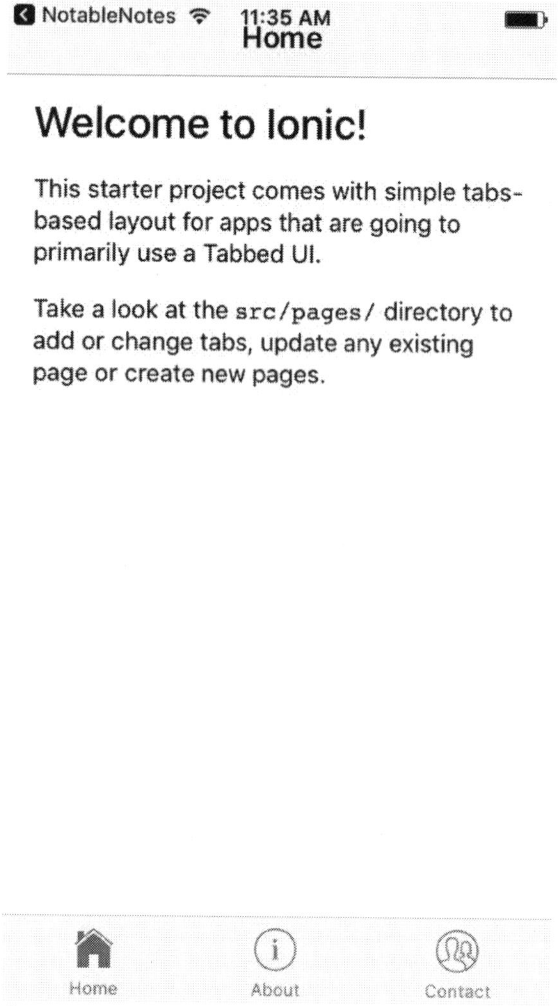

NotableNotes
11:35 AM
Home
Welcome to Ionic!
This starter project comes with simple tabs-based layout for apps that are going to primarily use a Tabbed UI.
Take a look at the src/pages/ directory to add or change tabs, update any existing page or create new pages.
Home
About
Contact

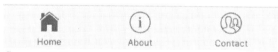

figure 10.2.1

We can navigate between three tabs, Home, About and Contact. In app.module.ts, we import four pages, we have three pages for each tab and one page (TabsPage) that serves as the container for our application.

In the *pages* directory, we find four additional directories: about, contact, home and tabs. In each directory are the html, scss and .ts files that define each tab.

With a general understanding of the structure of a tab-based Ionic application, we will start to modify our app.

app.module.ts

To begin using the camera plugin, we have to first import it in app module.

```
import { Camera } from '@ionic-native/camera';
```

and also add it to our *providers* array:

```
  providers: [
    StatusBar,
    SplashScreen,
    Camera,
    {provide: ErrorHandler, useClass: IonicErrorHandler}
  ]
```

about.html

Next in about.html, add the following in bold:

```
<ion-content padding>
  <button ion-button color="light" (click)="onTakePhoto()" round>Take Photo
  </button>
</ion-content>
```

We add a 'Take Photo' button that calls *onTakePhoto()* when it is clicked. We then implement *onTakePhoto* in about.ts as shown below:

```
import { Component } from '@angular/core';
import { NavController } from 'ionic-angular';

import { Camera, CameraOptions } from '@ionic-native/camera';

@Component({
  selector: 'page-about',
  templateUrl: 'about.html'
})
export class AboutPage {

  imageUrl = '';
```

```
  constructor(public navCtrl: NavController,private camera: Camera) {
  }

  onTakePhoto(){
    const options: CameraOptions = {
      quality: 100,
      destinationType: this.camera.DestinationType.DATA_URL,
      encodingType: this.camera.EncodingType.JPEG,
      mediaType: this.camera.MediaType.PICTURE,
      sourceType: this.camera.PictureSourceType.PHOTOLIBRARY
    }

    this.camera.getPicture(options)
      .then((imageData) => {
      // imageData is either a base64 encoded string or a file URI
      // If it's base64:
        let base64Image = 'data:image/jpeg;base64,' + imageData; // why
need this line?
        this.imageUrl = base64Image;
      }, (err) => {
      // Handle error
      });
    }
}
```

Code Explanation

```
import { Camera, CameraOptions } from '@ionic-native/camera';
```

We first import *Camera* and *CameraOptions* from *ionic-native/camera*.

```
export class AboutPage {

  imageUrl = '';

  constructor(public navCtrl: NavController,private camera: Camera) {
  }
```

We declare a variable *imageUrl* that holds the url of the photo that we will select from the Camera library or take using the Camera later. We also inject *Camera* in the constructor.

```
  onTakePhoto(){
    const options: CameraOptions = {
      quality: 100,
```

```
            destinationType: this.camera.DestinationType.DATA_URL,
            encodingType: this.camera.EncodingType.JPEG,
            mediaType: this.camera.MediaType.PICTURE,
            sourceType: this.camera.PictureSourceType.PHOTOLIBRARY
    }
```

We then proceed to implement *onTakePhoto*. We first declare a *const* variable *options* of type *CameraOptions*. *CameraOptions* are options that you want to pass to the camera. In our code, we go through a limited set of options as an example but you can read more about the available options in the Ionic documentation.

quality describes the quality of the saved image and is expressed as a range of 0-100, where 100 is typically full resolution with no loss from file compression. Typical values are 20, 50 and 100.

For *encodingType*, we choose the recommended type of encoding, JPEG. This can be changed to PNG.

For *sourceType*: we choose `this.camera.PictureSourceType.PHOTOLIBRARY` to get our picture from the Camera's photo library. If we want to take a picture instead, we change it to:

```
        sourceType: this.camera.PictureSourceType.CAMERA
```

getPicture

Having defined our camera options, we then pass these options to *getPicture*.

```
        this.camera.getPicture(options)
          .then((imageData) => {
            let base64Image = 'data:image/jpeg;base64,' + imageData;
            this.imageUrl = base64Image;
          }, (err) => {
            // Handle error
          });
        }
```

getPicture retrieves a photo from the device's image gallery because we have set *sourceType* to `this.camera.PictureSourceType.PHOTOLIBRARY`. It will take a photo using the camera if we used the `this.camera.PictureSourceType.CAMERA` option. The image is passed to the success callback as a Base64-encoded String, or as the URI for the image file.

Once the user snaps the photo or selects an existing image, the camera application closes and the application is restored.

The image value is sent to the callback function which we will render in an *<img>* tag in about.html.

about.html

In about.html, add the *img* tag as shown below.

```
<ion-content padding>
  <button ion-button color="light" (click)="onTakePhoto()" round>Take Photo
  </button>
  <img [src]="imageUrl">
</ion-content>
```

Having captured the *imageUrl*, we can choose to save the data locally using *Storage* or uploading the picture to a remote server or to Firebase. This however is beyond the scope of this book.

Running our App in the iOS Simulator

When we run our app in the Simulator and click on 'Take Photo', the Camera library will open for us to select our desired photo (fig. 10.2.2).

figure 10.2.2

After selecting our photo, we will be brought back to our app with the selected image being displayed (fig. 10.2.3).

figure 10.2.3

10.3 Using the Google Maps Plugin

Install angular2-google-maps

To display Google Map on our app, we will use an Angular plugin for Google Maps known as *angular2-google-maps*. Run the following command to add *angular2-google-maps* to our project:

```
npm install angular2-google-maps --save
```

app.module.ts

Import *AgmCoreModule* by adding the below code into app module.

119

```
import { AgmCoreModule } from 'angular2-google-maps/core';
```

Next, add *AgmCoreModule* to the *imports* array as shown below. Do note that you need to provide a Google Maps API key to be able to see a Map. You can obtain an API key at the Google Developers page at https://developers.google.com/maps/signup.

```
imports: [
    BrowserModule,
    IonicModule.forRoot(MyApp),
    AgmCoreModule.forRoot({
      apiKey: 'YOUR KEY'
    })
]
```

home.ts

Because we will be using the Google Map related plugins in the Home tab, in home.ts, declare two variables *lat* and *lng* to represent latitude and longitude respectively. Set it to the values as shown below. In case you are wondering, they are the latitude and longitude of my home country Singapore.

```
import { Component } from '@angular/core';
import { NavController } from 'ionic-angular';

@Component({
  selector: 'page-home',
  templateUrl: 'home.html'
})
export class HomePage {
  lat = 1.290270;
  lng = 103.851959;

  constructor(public navCtrl: NavController) {

  }
}
```

home.html

In home.html, add the below codes. *sebm-google-map* creates a google map on the page with the given *lat/lng* from the component as the initial center of the map with zoom value of 16 (you can try experimenting with different zoom values). *sebm-google-map-marker* adds a marker to the map at the given *lat/lng*.

120

```
<ion-content padding>

  <sebm-google-map
    [latitude]="lat"
    [longitude]="lng"
    [zoom]="16">
    <sebm-google-map-marker
      [latitude]="lat"
      [longitude]="lng">
    </sebm-google-map-marker>
  </sebm-google-map>

</ion-content>
```

home.scss

In home.scss, define the height for the *sebm-google-map* container. This is important. If not, the map will not be displayed on the page!

```
page-home {
    sebm-google-map{
        height:250px;

    }
}
```

Handling User Clicks

In this section, we learn how to handle user clicks on our map. Google maps has a *mapClick* event which is called when a user clicks on the map. We can handle it by adding it to the *sebm-google-map* component in home.html as shown below.

```
<sebm-google-map (mapClick)="onSetMarker($event)"
  [latitude]="lat"
  [longitude]="lng"
  [zoom]="16">
```

We then implement *onSetMarker* in home.ts:

```
onSetMarker(event){
  console.log(event);
  this.lat = event.coords.lat;
  this.lng = event.coords.lng;
```

121

```
    }
```

With the above code, we set *lat* and *lng* to the *lat* and *lng* provided in the *event* object. You might ask, how do I know that *lat* and *lng* is accessed via *event.coords?* An easy way is to print *event* to console (fig. 10.3.1).

figure 10.3.1

Note: You already know how to view the console if you are running your app via the Chrome browser. However, if you are running your in the iOS simulator, an easy way to view the console log is through the Safari console log. To access it, you need to first go to *Safari, Preferences, Advanced* and check the '*Show Develop menu in menu bar*'.

Once you have enabled the developer menu bar, go to *Develop, Simulator,* and go to *Console* to see the logs.

If you are running your app on the Android emulator, you can similar view the console in Chrome developer tools.

10.4 Geolocation

Next, we want to retrieve the current latitude and longitude of our device. We do this with the Geolocation plugin. Internally, the device determines its location via Global Positioning System (GPS) and location inferred from network signals such as IP address, RFID, WiFi and Bluetooth MAC addresses, and GSM/CDMA cell IDs.

We first install the plugins by running the below commands in Terminal:

```
ionic cordova plugin add cordova-plugin-geolocation
```

```
npm install --save @ionic-native/geolocation
```

app.module.ts

In app module, import *Geolocation* and also add it to *providers* array.

```
import { Geolocation } from '@ionic-native/geolocation';
```

```
providers: [
    ...

    ...
    Geolocation,
```

home.html

In home.html, add a button 'Locate' which calls *onLocate*.

```
<button ion-button color="light" (click)="onLocate()" round>Locate
</button>
```

home.ts

In home.ts, import *Geolocation* and inject it into the constructor.

```
import { Geolocation } from '@ionic-native/geolocation';

...

  constructor(public navCtrl: NavController,
            private geolocation: Geolocation) {

  }
```

Implement *onLocate* as shown:

```
onLocate(){
  this.geolocation.getCurrentPosition().then((resp) => {
    this.lat = resp.coords.latitude;
    this.lng = resp.coords.longitude;
```

```
    }).catch((error) => {
       console.log('Error getting location', error);
    });
   }
}
```

getCurrentPosition returns a Promise that resolves with the position of the device, or rejects with an error.

Running your App

If you run your app now and click on 'Locate', the map will show your current position.

Summary

In this chapter, we looked at how Cordova bridges the gap between the native layer and the web technology layer. We covered the steps to install a Cordova plugin and using it, in particular the Camera, Google Map and Geolocation plugin. With this plugin architecture, we can access more native device features in our applications.

CHAPTER 11: DEPLOYING TO THE APPSTORE

In this chapter, we will explore how to use the same Ionic code base and create the different versions that can be submitted to the various app stores. Before we deploy our app, make sure that the app metadata has been configured in config.xml (e.g. app id, name, description) as covered in chapter five.

11.1 Publishing the App in the Google Play Store

We first cover the steps of publishing an app to the Google Play Store and in the next section, publishing to the Apple App Store.

Build Preparations and Building for Production

As covered in chapter five, first ensure that we have added the platforms which we want to build our app for. Remember that the command to add a platform for Android is:

```
ionic cordova platform add android
```

Recall that to generate the necessary icons and splash screen images for the added platform, we run *ionic resources*.

Once all app metadata and resources are ready, we build our app for production by running:

ionic cordova build --release -prod android

This build process will be similar to the build process we used in development but it will also strip out debugging functionality and optimize our app for deployment.

Generating a Key

Once the build for Android is done, you can find your unsigned APK file in *platforms/android/build/outputs/apk/android-release-unsigned.apk*

We now need to sign the unsigned APK. To sign it, first generate our signing key with the *keytool* command installed with the JDK. For example:

keytool -genkey -v -keystore my-release-key.keystore -keyalg RSA -keysize 2048 -validity 10000 -alias my-

alias

Note: You can change *my-release-key.keystore* to your own filename.

When you run the command, you will be prompted a series of questions and lastly, to enter a key password. Once that is done, you will have the my-release-key.keystore file in the directory where you ran the keytool command.

Impt: Store the keystore file in a safe location. If you sign and submit an app with a keystore, all updates to that app must be signed with the same keystore.

Signing our APK with the Keystore

To sign our APK with the keystore, use the jarsigner tool (command below) included with the JDK:

jarsigner -verbose -sigalg SHA1withRSA -digestalg SHA1 -keystore my-release-key.keystore android-release-unsigned.apk alias_name

The command will ask you for the password you used to generate the keystore. When you enter the password, it will sign the application.

Optimizing the APK

Finally, run the zip align tool to optimize the APK. To align *android-release-unsigned.apk* and save it as *outfile.apk*, run the command:

zipalign -v <alignment> android-release-unsigned.apk outfile.apk

Note: The <alignment> is an integer that defines the byte-alignment boundaries. This must always be 4 (which provides 32-bit alignment) or else it effectively does nothing.

Once this is done, the release ready outfile.apk is ready to be submitted to the Google Play Store.

Submitting to the Google Play Store

To submit to Google Play, we first need to have a Google Developer account which has a one time fee of $25. After you have signed up for the account, you can sign in to the developer console and begin submitting your app which should be straightforward. Make sure to follow all the instructions like submitting app screenshots, app descriptions etc and your application should be available on the Google Play Store in a few hours.

11.2 Publishing the App in the Apple AppStore

Firstly, we need a paid Apple developer account which cost $99 per year.

Make sure that you have added *ios* as a platform (*ionic cordova platform add ios*) and built it (*ionic cordova build --release -prod ios*). In the *project/platforms/ios* folder generated by the build process, open the *.xcodeproj* file in Xcode.

In the Xcode project under *General*, make sure that *Team* is assigned (fig. 11.2.1).

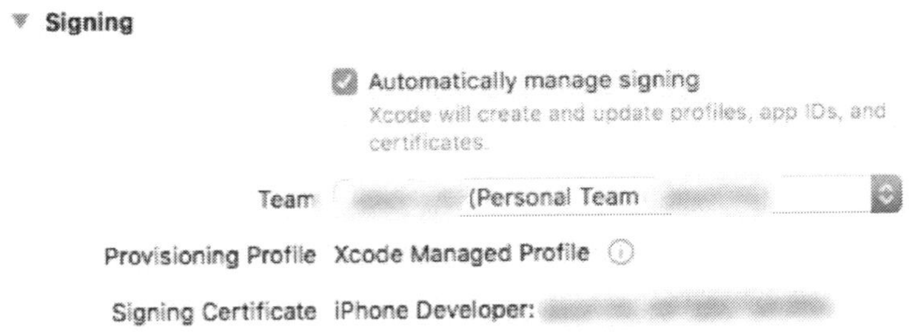

▼ **Signing**

    ☑ Automatically manage signing
      Xcode will create and update profiles, app IDs, and
      certificates.

    Team   (Personal Team   ⬍

Provisioning Profile Xcode Managed Profile ⓘ

Signing Certificate iPhone Developer:

figure 11.2.1

Next, under 'Preferences', 'Accounts', 'Manage Certificates', add 'iOS App Store' signing certificate and click 'done'. You should be allowed to do this if your account is a paid developer account (fig. 11.2.2).

figure 11.2.2

Next, go to https://developer.apple.com/account/ and click on *Certificates, IDs & Profiles*.

figure 11.2.3

You will see the certificates that you have created back in Xcode (fig. 11.2.3).

iTunesConnect

In the developer account, we only manage our certificates and identifiers used to sign our app. In iTunesConnect (https://itunesconnect.apple.com/), we manage the actual application to deploy to the app store. Login to iTunesconnect with your Apple id and click on 'My Apps' (fig. 11.2.4).

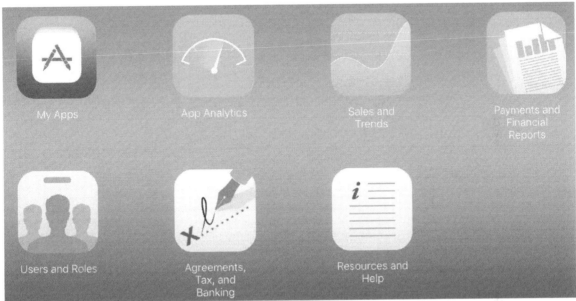

figure 11.2.4

Click on the '+', and select 'New App'. Fill in the fields (fig. 11.2.5).

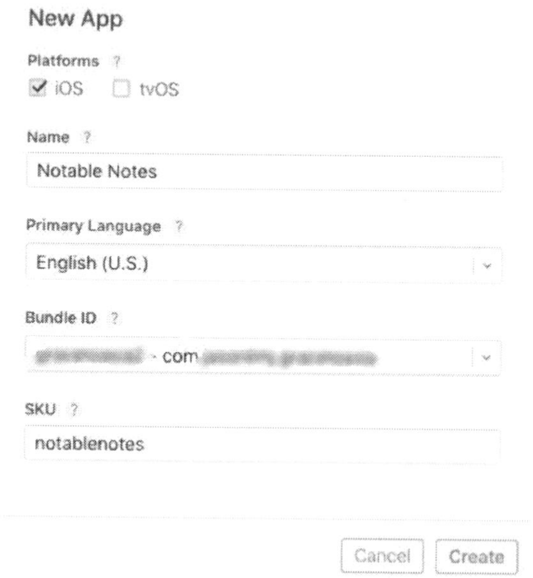

New App

Platforms ?
☑ iOS   ☐ tvOS

Name ?

Notable Notes

Primary Language ?

English (U.S.)   ⌄

Bundle ID ?

██████████ · com ████████████████   ⌄

SKU ?

notablenotes

Cancel   Create

figure 11.2.5

Click 'Create' and you will be brought to the 'App Information' page. You can choose your pricing and availability. From this point on, it should be straightforward to follow the steps as provided on the website.

Generating Our Archive

Now, we need to go back to Xcode to generate an archive which holds our application. Go to *Product, Scheme, Edit Scheme, Archive (Release)*, and make sure that *Build Configuration* is set to *Release* (figure 11.2.6).

figure 11.2.6

At the top bar in Xcode, make sure that you configured build for 'Generic iOS Device' as shown below.

Then go to 'Product', 'Archive'. This will bundle your web app to be deployed to the app store.

In the process, you might encounter this error:

"Dependency Analysis Error
NotableNotes has conflicting provisioning settings. NotableNotes is automatically signed for development, but a conflicting code signing identity iPhone Distribution has been manually specified. Set the code signing identity value to "iPhone Developer" in the build settings editor, or switch to manual signing in the project editor.
Code signing is required for product type 'Application' in SDK 'iOS 10.3'"

If you do not encounter this error, you can skip to the next section.

But to fix this, go to your app and click on the general tab and uncheck automatic signing.

131

▼ **Signing**

☐ Automatically manage signing
Xcode will create and update profiles, app IDs, and
certificates.

Then go to 'Build Settings', and under Signing, specify your 'Development Team'.

Now, go to 'Product', 'Clean'.

Go back to General, and check 'Automatically manage signing' again. Make sure you have 'Team' selected.

Now, go back to 'Product', 'Archive'. Xcode should then successfully create a package of your application.

Uploading to the App Store

A window should be opened where you can click on 'Upload to App Store...' (figure 11.2.7)

figure 11.2.7

Choose your account, and select 'Upload'. Xcode will then push your app into the App store. You might be requested to allow access to your key store several times because Xcode will use it to sign your app. Allow the access.

You can then go back to iTunesConnect to finishing out other relevant app information like price for example and under 'iOS App – Prepare for Submission', click 'Submit for Review'. The app submission process is a bit tricky and there can be potential errors not explained in this book. But seek advice from online app development communities e.g. stackoverflow or email me (support@i-ducate.com) and you should be on your way to publishing your app for iOS.

Summary

You now know how to properly build and submit your apps to both the Apple App Store and the Google Play Store.

CHAPTER 12: DEPLOYING TO A WEB SERVER

Other then publishing an app to the various App stores, we can also publish our app as a web application; that is, we deploy it to a web server so that users can access it just like any other website. This is useful especially for apps that have both a mobile app and a website and they provide access to the same data like Evernote and Google Drive. So users can work on the same data either from a mobile or desktop platform. Do remember however that none of the Cordova plugins will function in a browser. But while a browser might not have the same capabilities as a native application have, today's browsers do support several key features like geolocation, notifications and offline storage.

To run our app on a remote webserver, we should not be running the *ionic serve* command on a public server as it starts a development server and is not intended for use in production. Besides, there is no need to install the Ionic CLI on a server because our app has been transpiled to HTML, CSS and Javascript files that can be run on any http web server (apache, Microsoft IIS etc.).

Rather, we first build our app with the *ionic-build* command:

```
npm run ionic:build
```

Similar to how we build an Angular web app, this command compiles our Typescript code to Javascript and package it into a bundle using *webpack*. It then transforms the sass scss files into standard css files.

build generates its output in the *www* folder. Our entire application is contained in the folder. In it, we will find a *index.html* which looks like the one we have in *src* folder. It includes some Javascript files from the build sub folder. e.g. main.js file which contains all the Javascript code for our application. All our code is packaged into this single bundle. We can in fact open index.html as a file in our browser and it will run find as well.

We have so far done ran a development build. To run a more optimized production build, we run the following command:

```
npm run ionic:build —prod
```

Like the build for development, the production build too generates a *www* folder that contains everything required to run our app containing index.html, js, css files, *assets* folder, fonts and icons. We then take the generated *www* folder and deploy to the right location on a public server. As an example, we will show you how to deploy your app on Firebase hosting.

Deploying to Firebase Hosting

Although we are deploying to Firebase as an example, we can deploy to just any web server with similar procedures.

First, in the Firebase console, in the project that you have created, go to *Hosting* and click on *Get Started* (fig. 12.1).

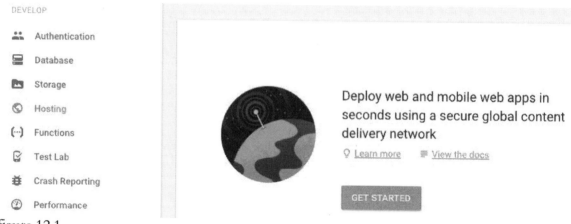

figure 12.1

A guide will appear telling you to install firebase tools as an *npm* package with the command *npm install -g firebase-tools* (fig. 12.2).

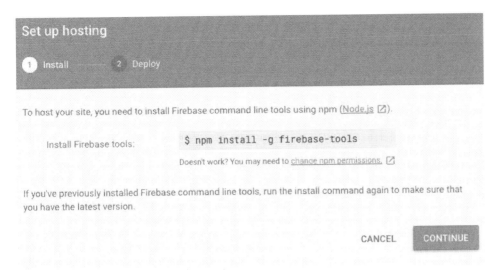

figure 12.2

Copy and paste this line into Terminal. Note that it has the -g flag which means firebase tools will be installed globally. When done, click continue.

The next screen tells you to sign in to firebase in Terminal using the command (fig. 12.3):

```
firebase login
```

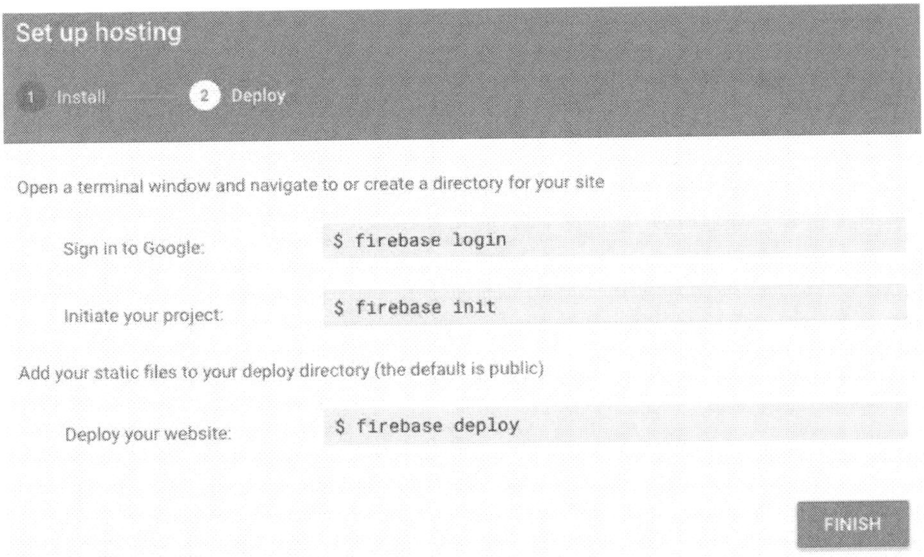

figure 12.3

Next, initialize your project by running

```
firebase init
```

This command adds some configuration files to your project.

You will next be prompted to choose which Firebase CLI features you want to setup. Choose the *Hosting* option (as shown below).

```
You're about to initialize a Firebase project in this directory:

  /Users/<your_username>/<your file location>/ionic/<your_project_name>

? Which Firebase CLI features do you want to setup for this folder? Press
Space
to select features, then Enter to confirm your choices. (Press <space> to
select
)
□□○ Database: Deploy Firebase Realtime Database Rules
 ○ Functions: Configure and deploy Cloud Functions
□○ Hosting: Configure and deploy Firebase Hosting sites
```

Next, choose the Firebase project you want to associate with.

Next specify which is our public directory. Enter *www* because that is the folder that contains all the files we want to serve as a public website.

Next, we have a question:

```
Configure as a single-page app (rewrite all urls to /index.html)? (y/N)
```

This option is useful for apps that use the Angular router but are not usually needed for Ionic apps. Since our app has a single page. We can answer 'N'.

For the next question, answer 'N'.:

```
File www/index.html already exists. Overwrite? (y/N) n
```

All these creates a *.firebaserc* file in your project folder which specifies which firebase project to use.

```
{
  "projects": {
    "default": "notablenotes-82b3d"  }
}
```

There is another file *firebase.json* where our public folder is configured to be *www*.

```
{
  "hosting": {
    "public": "www"
  }
}
```

The final step is to deploy our project using:

```
firebase deploy
```

In the Terminal, you should be provided a *Hosting URL* which your app will be hosted on. Your app will now be running live as a public website where people all over the world can access. We have used firebase hosting as an example, but you can upload the *www* folder to your own hosting service or web server for deployment there as well.

Summary

In this chapter, we learnt how to deploy our app onto a web server in particular, using Firebase hosting as an example.

CHAPTER 13: BUILDING A PROGRESSIVE WEB APP

There is a concept gaining traction called a progressive web app or *pwa*. Google in particular is pushing this with its Chrome browser. The basic idea behind a progressive web app is that a web app is able to be used by people as a regular web site on their phones initially and then they can use it more like a native mobile app progressively.

An advantage of progressive web apps is that it is discoverable, which means that their content can be discovered by search engines unlike native apps. They are also linkable. Users can link or bookmark within a *pwa* and return to it.

How It Works

Users would normally open a Chrome browser and navigate to a url. Suppose users like your app a lot and want to quickly launch it without going to the url every time. In the Chrome menu, they would click on the option 'Add to Home Screen' which adds a new launcher icon to the home screen. If one clicks on the icon, the app is launched except that there is no address bar at the top, just like a native app.

The emphasis here is that we started using our app as a website in Chrome and now we break free from the browser itself and can launch the app from the device's home screen just like a native app.

Some key features of a *pwa* is that it should:

- be served via *https*. This depends not on our application code but on which host we deploy our app on. With Firebase hosting, we get *https* for free.

- pages should be responsive on tablets/mobile devices. Ionic provides for this exactly.

- the start *url* of the app should be able to start even without an internet connection.

- provide metadata for 'Add to Home Screen'. i.e. customize the metadata to show a customized icon and app name.

Web App Manifest

We will see how to configure the metadata used by web browsers when adding our app to the Home screen.

The *manifest.json* file in *src* folder (shown below) contains the metadata information of our app. This file follows the W3C specification for web apps. This file is generated by the Ionic CLI when we created our project.

```
{
  "name": "Ionic",
  "short_name": "Ionic",
  "start_url": "index.html",
  "display": "standalone",
  "icons": [{
    "src": "assets/imgs/logo.png",
    "sizes": "512x512",
    "type": "image/png"
  }],
  "background_color": "#4e8ef7",
  "theme_color": "#4e8ef7"
}
```

In index.html, we have *<link rel="manifest" href="manifest.json">* which tells the browser to load manifest.json.

Let's look at the properties in detail:

name - the name used for the application listing.

short_name - is the name displayed along the home screen icon.

start_url - is the entry point to your application, usually index.html.

display - tells Chrome how to display the web application. The options are: fullscreen, standalone, minimal-ui, or browser. Here is what each option does:

> *fullscreen*: the web application is shown without the Chrome browser and will take up the entire display area

- *standalone*: the web application is launched to look and feel more like a standalone native application. The Chrome browser will not be shown but can include other UI elements like status bar and/or back button.

- *minimal-ui*: the web application is shown with a minimal set of UI elements for controlling navigation (i.e. back, forward, reload)

- *browser*: the web application will be shown in the standard Chrome browser.

Typically, the best option for *pwas* is the *standalone* option.

icons – this array defines the icon url, size, and file type of the app icon. It is used by the home screen and task switcher to display the app icon.

background_color – this hex value defines the background color of the web application.

theme_color – this hex value defines the color of the status bar.

orientation – though not listed in the generated version of the manifest.json file, this property defines the default orientation for the application. It can be either portrait or landscape.

Try It Out

Try changing the manifest.json settings to include your own icon, app name and build/deploy your app again. Go to the url where your web application is hosted and click 'Add to Home screen'.

Notice in your phone that your icon and app name is now shown. And when you launch it, the app starts with a launch screen with your icon and full app name. Note also that there is no browser address bar at the top because our manifest sets *standalone* as display mode.

Service Workers

The last functionality we need to add to make our app a full progressive web app is adding offline support, that is, making our app work even without an Internet connection. Service workers do that by intercepting and rewriting all of our application's network request. This gives us the ability to provide cached responses when there is no data connection available.

Usually whenever a browser makes a http request, it sends the request directly through the network to a server somewhere on the internet. The server would then send back a response. A service worker is simply a script written in Javascript that is called every time the browser makes a http request. The browser instead of sending the request to the remote service, will pass it to our service worker script and we can do whatever we want in the script. In particular, because we are interested in offline support, if there is no internet connection, our service worker can return a response from the local cache. So even if we cannot connect to the server, we return a response by re-using what we received from the same server earlier. In this way, our app can work even when offline.

The service worker API is currently supported in Chrome, Firefox and Opera. At point of writing, Apple's WebKit team has it marked under consideration.

It is straightforward to add a service worker to our project because it has generated code for enabling it. In index.html, the below code is currently commented out:

```
<!-- un-comment this code to enable service worker
<script>
  if ('serviceWorker' in navigator) {
    navigator.serviceWorker.register('service-worker.js')
      .then(() => console.log('service worker installed'))
      .catch(err => console.error('Error', err));
  }
</script>-->
```

We simply uncomment these lines to enable our service worker.

In the code we uncommented, we call *serviceWorker.register* and pass in a file *service-worker.js*. If we run our app now, you will see service worker installed in the console. And in 'application' tab, will see a service worker activated and running.

The 'Developer Tools' panel provides useful tools for testing: we can tell Chrome to go offline so any network request will fail. And when we reload our app while offline, our app loads anyway because the service worker retrieves from the local cache. We describe more about the local cache in the following section.

service worker.js

We first examine the code for the service worker.

```
'use strict';
```

```
importScripts('./build/sw-toolbox.js');

self.toolbox.options.cache = {
  name: 'ionic-cache'
};

// pre-cache our key assets
self.toolbox.precache(
  [
    './build/main.js',
    './build/main.css',
    './build/polyfills.js',
    'index.html',
    'manifest.json'
  ]
);

// dynamically cache any other local assets
self.toolbox.router.any('/*', self.toolbox.cacheFirst);

// for any other requests go to the network, cache,
// and then only use that cached resource if your user goes offline
self.toolbox.router.default = self.toolbox.networkFirst;
```

Note that service-worker.js is a plain Javascript file. It is not Typescript like the rest of our code. Because the service worker is loaded by the browser independently from the rest of our app, we cannot use Angular or Ionic functions here.

We can also see the *cache storage* in developer tools. The service worker created a cache and we can see all the requests that have been cached (fig. 13.1).

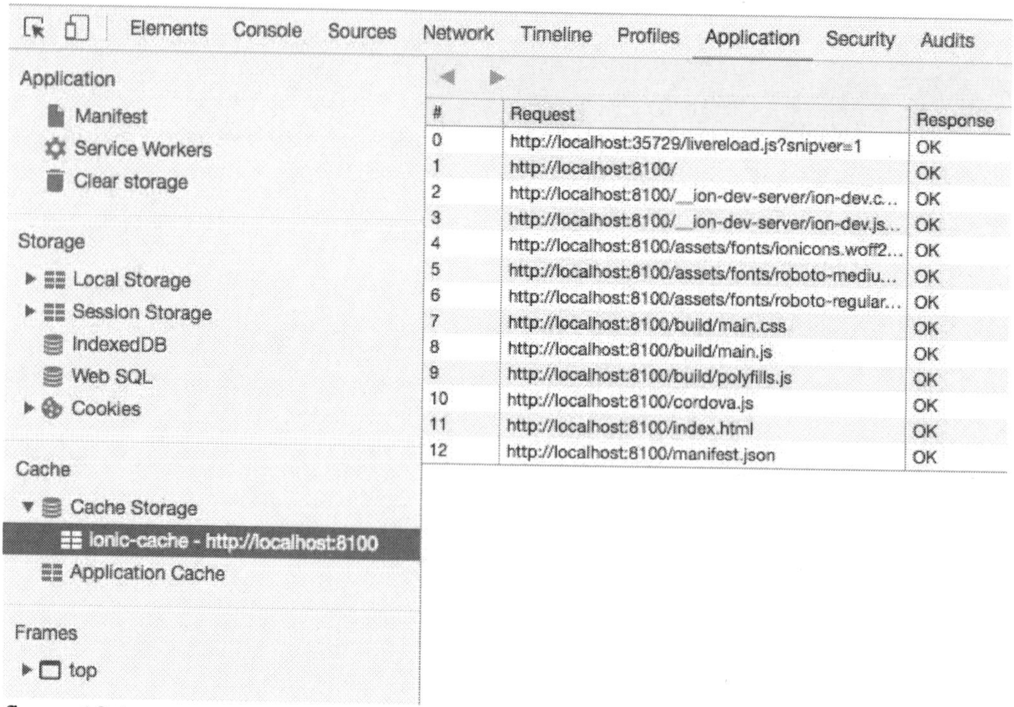

figure 13.1

The cache consists of key-value pairs. The request is the *key* in the cache. The response is the *value*. The Cache Storage contains all the files for our app starting from the index page, CSS files and Javascript files etc. It basically creates a local copy of our entire website so that our app can work offline. Note that by default, all files are cached. Note that this might not be always the right approach. For example, if you have other requests to other REST API to store/retrieve user data, you will probably need to tweak the service worker code. You might need to cache only some requests and not others or expire requests automatically after some time. In such a case, you need some smarter logic or else, you will end up with a huge cache. For now, caching everything is fine.

Now, build your app and deploy to Firebase hosting with the service worker enabled. When you run your app offline now, it should work.

Service workers help to improve the user experience of our app especially when there is no or poor Internet connectivity. Examine how much of your app functionality or content can be served locally where service workers can be implemented instead of making a network request.

Summary

In this chapter, we were introduced to the concept of Progressive Web Apps. We learnt how to release an app as a *pwa* and how to use Service workers to provide offline functionality. Support for *pwa*s will continue to grow with the Ionic Framework. So look out for enchancements over time.

With this knowledge, you can move on and build more complicated functional Ionic applications of your own!

Hopefully you've enjoyed this book and would like to learn more from me. I would love to get your feedback, learning what you liked and didn't for us to improve. Please feel free to email me at support@i-ducate.com if you encounter any errors with your code. Visit my GitHub repository at https://github.com/greglim81 if you have not already to have the full source code for this book.

If you didn't like the book, please email us and let us know how we could improve it. This book can only get better thanks to readers like you.

If you like the book, I would appreciate if you could leave us a review too.

Thank you and all the best to your learning journey in Ionic!

ABOUT THE AUTHOR

Greg Lim is a technologist and author of several programming books. Greg has many years in teaching programming in tertiary institutions and he places special emphasis on learning by doing.

Contact Greg at support@i-ducate.com.

APPENDIX A: THEMES

In this appendix, we learn about theming our Ionic app. To change our theme, we update our *src/theme/variables.scss* file. In this file, we can overwrite default colors and also other properties like fonts and so on. *variables.scss* is an scss file which stands for "Sassy CSS". Why Sassy? Its a pun on the term 'sass'. 'sass' stands for 'Syntactically Awesome Style Sheets'. Ionic uses *sass* for styling (see http://sass-lang.com/ for more on *sass*). *sass* is a *css* pre-processor which means that this form will be transformed by *sass* into regular *css* styles that will then be loaded by the browser. So a *scss* file is similar to a *css* file but it provides a more powerful syntax, for example, you can declare variables that you can use later in your styles. For example, we have *$colors* in variables.scss which define our colors as shown below:

```
$colors: (
  primary:    #488aff,
  secondary:  #32db64,
  danger:     #f53d3d,
  light:      #f4f4f4,
  dark:       #222
);
```

primary is set to *#488aff* which is the blue default color. We can change it to another color *rgb*. When we change and save it, the *ionic serve* process will compile all scss files to use our new variables values and the header bar color will change accordingly.

For example, we have a button set to the color of 'light'.

```
<button ion-button color="light" (click)="onLocate()" round>Locate
</button>
```

Currently, *light* is currently set to the color value of *#f4f4f4* in *$colors*. But suppose we want to set a new value for light, we can change it. In the below, we change *light* to be *pink*.

```
$colors: (
  primary:    #488aff,
  secondary:  #32db64,
  danger:     #f53d3d,
  light:      pink,
  dark:       #222
);
```

Notice how Ionic makes defining our own theme colors easy. With this, we can fully customize the theme of our app.

Made in the USA
San Bernardino, CA
18 July 2018